The Pre-Law Survival Guide

Save time, money, and stress on your legal journey

Jolene Blackbourn, Esq.

TABLE OF CONTENTS

FORWARD

The Calf Path

One day, through the primeval wood,
A calf walked home, as good calves should;
But made a trail all bent askew,
A crooked trial as all calves do.

Since then 200 years has fled,
And, I infer, the calf is dead.
But still he left behind his trial,
And thereby hangs my moral tale.

The trail is taken up next day
By a lone dog that passed that way;
And then a wise bell-weather sheep
Pursued the trial o'er vale and steep,
And drew the flock behind him, too,
As good bell-weathers always do.

And from that day, o'er hill and glade,
Through old those old woods a path was made;
And many men wound in and out,
And dodged, and turned, and bent about
And uttered words of righteous wrath
Because 'twas such a crooked path.
But still they followed-do not laugh-
The first migrations of that calf,
And through this winding wood-way stalked,
Because he wobbled when he walked.

This forest path became a lane,
That bent, and turned, and turned again;
This crooked lane became a road,
Where many a poor horse with his load
Toiled on beneath the burning sun,
And traveled some three miles in one.
And thus a century and a half
They trod the footsteps of that calf.

The years passed on in swiftness fleet,
The road became a village street;

And this, before men were aware,
A city's crowded thoroughfare;
And soon the central street was this
Of a renowned metropolis;
And men two centuries and a half
Trod in the footsteps of that calf.

Each day a hundred thousand rout
Followed the zigzag calf about;
And o'er his crooked journey went
The traffic of a continent.
A hundred thousand men were led
By one calf near three centuries dead.
They followed still his crooked way,
And lost one hundred years a day;
For thus such reverence is lent
To well-established precedent.

A moral lesson this might teach,
Were I ordained and called to preach;
For men are prone to go it blind
Along the calf-paths of the mind,
And work away from sun to sun
To do what other men have done.
They follow in the beaten track,
And out and in, and forth and back,
And still their devious course pursue,
To keep the path that others do.

But how the wise old wood-gods laugh,
Who saw the first primeval calf!
Ah! many things this tale might teach-
But I am not ordained to preach.

-Sam Walter Foss

INTRODUCTION

Throughout my legal journey I found that whenever I did something that wasn't recommended, I saved money. - Jolene Blackbourn

Many attorneys cannot afford to practice in their dream field because of overwhelming debt. By the end of this book, you'll know the steps to take to make your dream a reality.

Let me know if this sounds familiar. When I was a kid, I wanted to be many things, but I think, most of all, I wanted to be important, impressive, remembered.

In high school, I was an overachiever. One year I was on almost every page of the yearbook. I had multiple letters and got into a good university.

Somewhere along the way, law school became my focus. It had been floating in and out for some time but as college was coming to an end, I knew I wanted more education. I didn't want to go to med school. I wanted more direction than grad school. So, law school won by default.

Sure, there were a few other reasons to go. How else was I going to save the world?

I figured I could save the world but if that didn't work out, at least I had a designated career path. It didn't really matter that I had no idea what I would do as a lawyer. I figured I would be a transactional attorney and work as little as possible while making as much as possible. Sounds good, right?

I, like so many in this book and so many in the world, discovered that being an attorney is very different from what you see on TV. Many times, you don't get to choose what area of law you go into. Other factors like your debt load, need for better income, the economy, and your grades factor into whether you get to work in your chosen area of law. So many law students start law school with the intention of becoming a certain type of attorney but leave law school becoming a different type of attorney.

My question for you is, are you OK with that? Are you going to law school to live a very specific dream? Or will any area of law do? What have you done to make that dream a reality?

Most of us figure it will work out. I can tell you, even though I had dream internships and externships knocking on my door in my chosen field, I never got to practice in that field. Other factors took over. I tried. It's not like I settled for the first job offer. I practically went bankrupt trying to "live my dream." So, what are you doing to make your dream a reality? Do you even know what you have to do?

That's what this book is all about. Let's get you where you actually want to go. Let's set you up for success! In the end, that may not be law school. Or it may mean doing very particular things before law school, so you have offers knocking on your door in the area of law that you want to practice in before you graduate law school.

Over the first year of The Legal Learning Podcast, I placed my guests into six main categories, five of which are covered in this book. Those five categories are self-care, finances, practical tips, nontraditional students, and leaving law. The tips and strategies provided in these categories will provide you with knowledge many pre-law students of the past didn't have but really wished they had.

There is no need for students to go to law school without the guidance and advice of those who have walked that path before. The world is full of people who can make your journey easier. The Legal Learning Podcast was created to hand-deliver these stories and opportunities to you. Now these stories and opportunities are available here, in written form.

If any of the guests or strategies help you with your legal journey, please let me know. I would love an Instagram post tagging @legallearningcenter or #legallearningpodcast or send an email to Jolene@LegalLearningCenter.Com.

A list of resources mentioned in this book is available in the back of this book for your convenience. Please note that any quotes contained in this book may actually be paraphrased from conversations held on The Legal Learning Podcast but all meaning and content have been maintain.

PART 1

PART 1: LAW AND FINANCES

Law students tend to fall into one of two categories: those who see the large law loans looming and bulldoze ahead with blinders on, and those who refuse to take out law loans at all costs. Students can make poor decisions in either boat by being too extreme. The key is to find balance between the student loans of undergrad and law school. - Jolene Blackbourn

By the time we're in college, we know that to reach our goals, we need a plan. In high school, the plan was to get good grades, volunteer, and join activities so that colleges would like us. In college, we make a similar plan to get into the next level of our education. The problem with creating the same plan for higher education is the debt load can be so much more, yet students rarely make much of a financial plan. The focus is, get good grades and hope for scholarships.

It's rare for someone to seek financial planning advice before they have a full-time job. Their financial decisions are based on the few tips they're exposed to. For example, they may start college at a community college to save money. Or they take a few advance placement tests to save money. But that's the extent of their financial strategies.

When it comes to law school, the big financial strategy is to get the best LSAT score possible. This is a mistake. There are lots of ways to save on the educational journey, but rather than uncover them, students are oftentimes so busy trying to get to the next step in their plan, law school, that they fail to slow down and make a financial plan, and they certainly don't consult with a financial advisor.

That financial plan can be vital to living the life they always dreamed of as an attorney. Many attorneys are drowning in debt and their income isn't what they thought it would be. Some find that their nonlawyer friends are making better income than they are, once that debt-to-income ratio is factored in. But this doesn't have to be the case.

It has long been the theory of law students that they will simply take out the loans and pay them back once they start working. Students often have some type of vague accelerated repayment plan in mind. Unfortunately, these students don't have an exact plan and don't understand how little they might actually be making when they graduate. The lack of substantial income makes accelerated repayment difficult. Additionally, for most loans, interest is accruing while they're in school, adding thousands to their repayment total. Therefore, it's best to avoid loans in the first place. Again, students rarely make a plan to do so.

As I prepared for law school, the only financial advice I was given was "Live like a lawyer while you're a law student and you'll live like a law student while you're a lawyer." Basically, take out student loans, live frugally as a student, and I would be fine. I was assured I would be able to pay back my loans once I started working. This was the worst advice ever. After many years of living in debt and anger, I did a little research and discovered why so many people gave me such bad advice.

I'm at the tail end of Gen X. It turns out that the advice I received was good for those who were giving it to me, namely Baby Boomers and early Gen Xers. When those people went to law school, it was actually affordable.[1] For many of them, they never needed to practice law in order to pay back their loans. They could literally attend law school, never pass the bar exam, and still have a decent life as long as they had a decent paying job. However, starting with the second half of Gen X, the cost of law school started to rise to the point that living frugally as a law student really didn't make a dent in the debt load and taking out the offered student loans meant drowning in debt as a lawyer.

Let me just show you a few numbers. In 1985, the average law school tuition for an in-state public school attendee, according to the American Bar Association, was $2,006. By 2012 that figure went up to $23,214. That would be fine if income matched. However, in looking at the median household income during that timeframe (so keep in mind this is everyone, not just lawyers), income increased from $54,334 to 57,623.[2]

Of course, if you attended private school, the numbers are even worse. In 1985 you could still attend private school and never practice as an attorney. In 2012 you were drowning in debt.

In 1985 students could pay for three years of private law school tuition with just 40% of their annual income. In 2012, three years of private law school tuition cost over two years of salary.

1985

Average in-state public tuition	$2,006
Average private tuition	$7,526
Median Household Income	$54,334

2012

Average in-state public tuition	$23,214
Average private tuition	$40,634
Median Household Income	$57,623

Obviously, these numbers haven't improved over time.

But let's take a look at attorney salaries. The mean income of an attorney as of 2020. While it tends to increase each year, it's not as high as you might think, especially after taking out approximately $150,000 in loans.

Pay particular attention to the lower end of the spectrum. A huge number of students are making between $50,000-$80,000. And this isn't a chart of starting salaries, this is a chart of all attorneys, new and in practice for 20 plus years.

You may try to convince yourself that you won't fall into that $50,000 range, but there are a lot of areas of law that pay fairly low, so it's best to have a plan. Many attorneys start off earning in the $60,000-$70,000 range. In fact, I had two colleagues in Los Angeles who graduated nine years apart. After graduation they went into similar areas of law. Despite nine years of tuition hikes, they both had the same starting salary, $60,000. If that's a general starting salary in an expensive city like Los Angeles, just be prepared for a potentially lower starting salary if you're in a smaller town.

The following is a chart of lawyer salaries in 2020.[3]

Distribution of Reported Full-time Salaries – Class of 2020

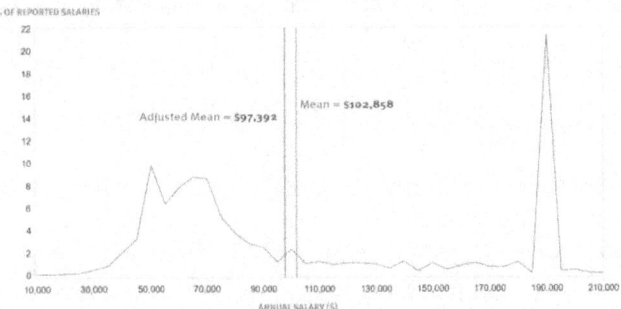

In order to afford law school and live a decent life after, prospective law students need to approach their legal journey strategically to avoid an overwhelming debt-to-income ratio.

Let's look at a specific example.

The median starting salary for law school graduates is $72,500.[4] Assuming you make that amount and yet have $150,000 in student loans, it will be very difficult to pay all your bills. Just to make the figures clear: With a salary of $72,500, your monthly gross income is $6061.66. You'll need to subtract your state income tax rate, if any (In California, you would need to take out about $1,500 in state income tax each month), then subtract your loan payment ($150,000 at 5% interest rate over 20 years repayment term = $990 per month) and don't forget your rent! Again, in California your rent can easily be $2,000 a month. This leaves you with $1577.66 (approximately) for all your federal taxes, utilities, car expenses, fun, other necessities, and, dare I suggest, savings, or even children? Obviously, these numbers will vary by location and person. But this gives you an idea of how tight a budget crunch many attorneys find themselves.

Making a financial plan with someone who's an expert before you incur student debt can really make a difference in your future. Even if you don't engage the services of a financial coach until after law school, doing so from the very beginning of your career, once you're making a little money, will make a huge difference. Again, do this even if you feel like you have no money or time to spare, it could literally change your future!

Lawyers tend to be perfectionists. We don't like to show anyone our weak side. In fact, we're trained to not admit we have a weak side. But when it comes to finances, we need to ignore that. We need to push through that barrier and get the advice we actually need. The sooner you do it, the more financially successful your future will be.

To be clear, this isn't just applicable to those with "low" starting salaries. If you're making good money from day one, you should do this as well. It's okay to not know everything. It's okay to need some guidance. It's okay to make mistakes! Just don't let them continue. Your knowledge is about law. When you're dealing with finances (especially the size of law loans) seek out someone with finance/student loan knowledge. It's not a weakness to seek help in an area in which you have no training; it's a strength!

So where do you find a financial guru? There are a lot of them out there. I would start by listening to debt-reduction or debt-avoidance podcasts. But it goes beyond that. You need strategies about what to do if a lump sum of money comes in, such as a bonus. Do you pay off a debt, pay down a larger debt, or pay cash for a new car that you know you'll need soon anyway? That advice will differ from advisor to advisor. Here are a few thoughts. Talk to an advisor and get an idea of their theories. See if their theories and their systems make sense to you. You may be working with this person for a while, so make sure you like working with them, and make sure they understand you!

The most consistent advice I received from the various financial expert guests on The Legal Learning Podcast was that it's never too soon to seek financial help. If you're not making much money, if you're drowning in debt, or, if you're about to embark on a change in your journey, whether that means you're changing your path or perhaps about to start law school, it's a good idea to check in with a financial coach and make sure that you're on track to reach your life goals. Check the list of resources at the end of this book for more information.

CHAPTER 1: GAP YEARS

If one of your goals as an attorney is to be secure financially, the best way to do that is gap years. I know many students don't want to take time off. They're afraid they'll lose motivation. They don't want to fall behind their peers who may be headed to law school. They don't want to pay the extra money if tuition increases. But in this chapter, I'll show you how taking just a few gap years can save you hundreds of thousands of dollars, help your mental health, and make you more attractive to employers and internships.

Let's start with advice from some financial experts who were guests on The Legal Learning Podcast.

Financial coach Christine Teh had to delay her college experience so that she could gain residency and lower the cost of her education. Many students delay their education for financial or family reasons. However, many of us are so focused on becoming attorneys as fast as possible that we refuse to slow down. We don't even acknowledge that there are plenty of students who graduate from law school "later" in life. All we see are those who graduate by age twenty-six and we feel like a failure if we don't accomplish that for ourselves. It's important to take the time to reflect on why we feel so rushed and whether those reasons are in our best interest.

I didn't want to be in debt, so I was working full-time and going to school at night. It took me longer to get my degree. I probably got my degree at 26-years-old 'cause I was going part-time, working full-time. Plus, the first year, I couldn't go to school mainly because as a non-California resident, they were charging $100 per unit versus $10 per unit; that was a big difference for me. So I didn't go to school for the first year; I just worked. So, I didn't finish until 26 and then I was working full-time, and then I didn't have a life. It wasn't the most fun.

Of course, if you can afford to, maybe go to school and then maybe kind of work on the side, maybe do full-time and then just figure out how you can lower your financial burden. There are always options like working as much as possible to avoid student loan debt.

Or just suck it up and just live with your parents. It's not forever. I know we're in a society where, "Oh, we want something right now, right now, right now. I don't wanna live with my parents", but just think, it's just temporary, and money is important. As much as you don't wanna believe it. Money is important; you have to embrace and accept that.[5]

Once we acknowledge that not everyone graduates from law school at twenty-six years old, we can look into the benefits of gap years. The most practical of the benefits is that if you take gap years with the intent to save for law school, you could save enough to pay cash for all, or even half, of law school within a handful of years.

The average college student starting salary is over $50,000.[6] The average law student takes out $160,000 in loans.[7] Assuming the student must pay $50,000 a year for their legal education, it would take 4 years if the student saved $1,000 a month. This is something I was able to do while living at home with my dad and making only $24,000 (a million years ago). Meagan, the very first guest on The Legal Learning Podcast was able to save $1,000 a month, while making around $35,000 a year and not living at home.[8]

If you're making $50,000, would it be possible to save $2,000 a month? Could you then pay cash for your first year of law school in just two years? If you worked side jobs on top of your regular job, could you save even more. In just three gap years, saving $2,000 a month, you could pay cash for almost half of law school! Once combined with a handful of other money-saving techniques I teach my students, law school could easily be paid for without much effort.

Ultimately, it's just a matter of simple math. Using very basic numbers and national averages:

$50,000 income = $4,000 income a month.
$2,000 saved per month for two years is just under $50,000.

If law school is $50,000 per year, you can pay for a year of law school in two years.

Using these numbers (assuming no raises or large expenses), you could pay cash for law school in six years.

Here's the big secret. Saving $50,000 isn't just saving $50,000. Students actually pay anywhere from 20% to 80% of their student loan total, in interest! So, $150,000 in student loans means a repayment of approximately $225,000. If you're one of those students with $100,000 in undergrad debt, and you take out another $100,000 in law school, you're looking at $300,000 in repayment.

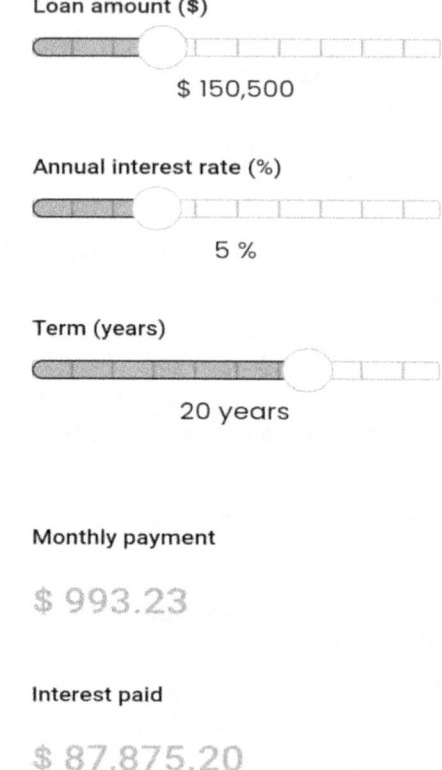

Loan amount ($)

$ 150,500

Annual interest rate (%)

5 %

Term (years)

20 years

Monthly payment

$ 993.23

Interest paid

$ 87,875.20

By avoiding $50,000 in loans, you're avoiding $75,000 in repayment. So, saving even just one year's worth of tuition could literally change your entire trajectory. So, really ask yourself, what's the rush? And can you live at home like Christine? Can you save like Meagan?

Another benefit to gap years is work experience. Many try to work for a law firm to "gain experience." The problem is that no law firm is really going to give you "lawyer" experience. Sure, you'll be in a firm, and if you're there long enough, you may be given some valuable responsibilities. But if you're only there for a year or two, you might as well be working in any office.

To really maximize your gap year(s), I recommend you attempt to work in another area of interest for you, while keeping in mind that part of your goal is to save money, so you don't want to take the lowest paying job out there.

Most people have multiple interests. They may be interested in art and law. Or environmental law. Could you spend your gap years working in an art-related job? Or at an environmental nonprofit? There are two reasons I recommend this over a law firm job.

First, you can explore a potential career field that doesn't cost $150,000. If you find your dream job while saving up money, what's the worst that can happen? You're happy and you have savings! You can now buy a car or a house, perhaps. And law school is still there if you want it later.

Second, if you get experience in an area of interest related to law, you can network, learn what it's really like in the field. This can greatly improve your chances of getting a great internship while in law school and a job thereafter. Competition is tough for good internships. A person with any work experience tends to have an edge on the competition. But a person who has experience and connections is well set up for success.

Alternatively, you may decide a different area of law is better for you. You may discover you don't actually like that community or the pay associated with it. Many law students spend their first law school summer in an internship that they thought they wanted, only to discover it's exactly what they don't want. This gap year work experience can literally save you time and money while in law school, as you'll have a better idea of what you want.

The goal isn't to rush through life as fast as possible. The goal is to be happy. If you enjoy taking gap years, that's okay. If you want to take a few more, that's okay too. There's nothing wrong with that. In fact, if you take gap years you may be a better law student because your brain has had a chance to rest. You're refreshed. You're ready to be a student again. If you have senioritis in college, it's only going to get worse when you have to work twice as hard in law school! You don't have to kill yourself to be a lawyer by twenty-six years old! Take a deep breath, slow down, and really evaluate the benefits of gap years before dismissing them like so many do.

CHAPTER 2: MAKE MORE MONEY

Whether you take gap years or not, the more money you make, the more you can save or avoid loans. I interviewed Nick Loper, host of the top-rated podcast The Side Hustle Show in order to chat about how a student, who is too busy to work (especially during their 1L year) can make some money. He shared a handful of ideas from his nine years of podcasting.[9]

These projects fall into three categories. Those that can be done almost passively, those that may require some start-up attention but can be passed off, and those that you could do sporadically. The key is to find something that will work for your lifestyle and commitments. If your goal is to change your financial trajectory, it's important that while you may try some of these ideas, if they aren't helping you with that goal, you may need to simply move on.

<u>Print On Demand</u>

You can design items whether it is a digital print out or a product design and have it set up in a way that the product automatically ships or can be printed when the customer completes the purchase. You don't need to complete the order.

Printables are often sold on Etsy and can be things like a law school application checklist, a dorm room cleaning schedule, or a birthday party game. Printables are basically anything that a customer can print out and would want for practical or entertainment purposes.

Likewise, if you had a variety of designs that could be applied to t-shirts, folders, backpacks, and so forth and were only created when ordered by a customer, you can use a company to take care of the entire process so that you'd simply receive the profit. A few companies that do this are Society6, Amazon, and RedBubble. You have probably ordered a print-on-demand product from one of these companies in the past.

Service-Based Businesses

While service businesses may require you to actually work in the business, you can potentially hire an employee to replace you if you become too busy or no longer wish to do the business. A few examples of a service-based business are maid service, dog poop clean up, rain gutter cleaning, car windshield repair, and so forth.

It's anything that people need done but don't want to do or don't have time to do. You could start out working weekends. As your clientele grows, you can hire someone to replace you. So, for example, if you had a business up and running before your 1L year, you could potentially manage it without too much effort. You would have your worker performing the services you used to perform. So, if you were cleaning homes for $80 and you hired someone for $60 per home, you could make $20 per home while not working. You would just be in charge of scheduling and complaints. Regardless of your actual numbers, making money while not really working is always nice.

Along the same lines, there's always a need for people with tech skills. You may not have any skills in this area but there are a lot of classes out there that can help you develop a very specific set of skills quickly. For example, if you want to learn how to build a website on a particular platform like Wix, you could then grow a clientele just for that. Or Salesforce has a free training program. If you learned an attorney billing program and how to service it, you could not only help clients now, but also be the first choice among your classmates if they start their own firms. As you begin to practice law, you could be making side money helping friends learn and manage their billing systems. Check it out and see if that's something you could do.

Become an expert in one thing and become known for that thing. Typically, college and law students work ten to twenty hours a week and make very little money. Website developers and other tech people make a lot more in a lot less time. Even if they don't get as much work, just think of all the free time they have to put toward their studies or toward attending networking events or anything else they want to do.

If you develop these tech skills while still in college, you could take gap years and offer these services on the side, thereby increasing your savings toward law school. You could offer them during law school and make money when others may feel too busy to work. And, as a lawyer, you could still offer these services and pay off your debt faster.

Flipping

Another great way to make money while you're in law school with little commitment is flipping items. Find free or cheap furniture (or other items), fix it up and sell it on the Nextdoor app or Facebook Marketplace or whichever app seems to work best for your neighborhood. You can even trade it for profit.

The trade up idea can start with items from your home that you're no longer using, so for example, if you have an old Kindle, can you trade it for a Chromebook? Trade the Chromebook for a regular computer and so forth. Sell when you get to a point where you would like the cash.

There's a whole trading industry where people make profits from their trades. I know you may wonder who would make the trades I just listed, but it simply depends on what people want or need. I've tried trading and was able to exchange a five-gallon fish tank for a computer with Windows 10 on it! You just never know.

There is a huge industry in flipping items that are obtained for free off Craigslist or items found at garage sales. This is something that you can do whenever you have time and drop it when you don't have time. You can do it during school vacations and stop doing it when you're in school.

Content Creation

A lot of students want to start a blog or a vlog about their legal journey. That's a great idea. However, if you're using that to make money, please note that that's generally a much slower way to make money than the above listed items. This idea also has a lot of potential repercussions because the information is public. If you say the wrong thing or if you're not a great writer, future employers may see this. If you share gossipy items, this could cause problems in getting a job. You, therefore, need to be professional at all times.

You need to understand what your goal is in creating the blog or vlog. I would suggest that you do research on how to monetize a blog or vlog before you get started if that's actually your goal. Speaking with students who've already done this is important if monetization is your goal. Sara of Cerebellum-Chef.com shared her experience blogging in law school, which I highly recommend you listen to if this is something you're considering. Just to give you a little insight into that interview, aside from understanding SEO...

So, if you're planning on trying to monetize your advice, then you're gonna have to go the extra mile and look up all of the different websites that you can get stock images from and figure out how to set up your Pinterest buttons and make sure that everything is clickable. I do that, but it's taken a lot of practice and it adds more time. It's not just writing something down; it then becomes a four-hour venture in making sure that all of these images line up the way you want them to, and that they actually... If you click on them, don't send you to a different website, you wanna make sure they pop up outside in a separate tab, so people are still on your site reading, and then you also have to make sure that you have an affiliate link information piece at the bottom of your blog, and so you kinda start dabbling a little bit in law because you want make sure that you're not using trademark infringement of images and that you're making sure people understand that you might get paid if they click on affiliate links, all those things kind of intertwine. So, it becomes a little bit more hectic.[10]

The key to making more money is to choose something and be specific about it. Do some research on your choice and really learn about it, so you're not stuck with a minimum-wage on-campus job, so you're not stuck with your nine-to-five post-graduate job. You don't have to work a lot of hours to make good money. Work smarter, not harder!

CHAPTER 3: STUDENT LOANS

The reality is, most students, even if they save extra money, need to take out some student loans. If you do need to take out student loans, you should do so strategically. Most people think that they just need to go to the bank and take out a student loan when it comes time to take out a private loan. However, if you approach this strategically, you could save thousands. For example, Juno is a company that negotiates lower rates on private student loans by doing so in bulk.

Similar to saving money by buying in bulk at Costco, Juno puts together a group of students who are in a similar situation, meaning they're applying for a law loan and have a similar credit score. Juno can negotiate a better rate this way than the students can on their own. In fact, sometimes, students get a lower interest rate on their private loan through Juno than what the federal government offers. These loans have no origination fees and are often able to offer cash back as well.

Another way to use Juno is to refinance your loans. Once you've taken out your loans, you can refinance as often as you like. This could also save you thousands over the life of your loan. Yet many students never take advantage of this. When the founders of Juno originally negotiated their own loans, they saved, on average, $15,000! For a link directly to the law related information, visit advisor.legallearningcenter.com/juno.[11]

Default and Deferment

The reality is that somewhere around 20% of students are in default on their student loans.[12] Obviously no one does that intentionally. We all go to law school thinking we're improving our financial situation. But between large student loans, comparatively low income, and occasionally a bad economy, it can be very difficult to make those payments.

Lenders offer deferments. This is an option to place your student loan payments on hold while you try to get back on your feet. However, if you put your loans into deferment, the interest still accrues for unsubsidized loans.[13] When you're ready to restart your payments, the interest that accrued during the deferment is rolled into the principal. That interest that accrued is now part of the principal. You're now required to pay interest on top of that new total. So, you're placed in a worse financial situation for needing that break from paying. Many times, this really hinders attorneys from successfully getting back on their feet.

Twenty-five percent of students who default on their student loans, default a second time within five years. Additionally, borrowers who participate in income-driven repayment plans for the purpose of having some of their loans forgiven, lose access to that program and their benefits while in default. This means if they were close to having their loans forgiven, that timeline is extended. Borrowers may be charged up to 25% of the principal and interest while that interest continues to accrue. They can also be charged fees in some circumstances.[14]

Student loans are generally not waived in bankruptcy. However, recently, there have been a few court cases that allowed people to discharge their loans in their bankruptcy. It's very case specific and very difficult to achieve. However, if that's the trend, it's something to keep your eye on. While it is never a place you want to be, it's good to know your options, should you need them.

Regardless of whether you ever default or defer, it's important to avoid student loan debt to allow flexibility in your future. You never know what the future may hold. You may have a spouse who suddenly becomes injured, and you need to care for them. You may have children with special needs, and you need to take time off work or work a reduced schedule to take care of them. One of your parents may need extra care that you would like to provide. Or it could be something as simple as you don't really like the area of law that you went into, and you want to explore another area of law that will most likely require a pay cut. And in some more dramatic cases, you may even want to leave the practice of law.

All of the above scenarios require savings. It's a lot easier to accomplish these goals without significant student loans. Many students pay $1,000 to $2,000 a month toward their student loans. At that amount, there's no room for pay cuts or sabbaticals. Most of us go to law school to expand our options in life; to have more opportunities. However, many attorneys discover they have, in fact, limited their opportunities in life by taking on so much debt.

Along those lines, President Biden has talked about student loan forgiveness. The amount of that forgiveness keeps changing. Additionally, the money continues to not come. I would find a change in the bankruptcy code to be a more likely way out of student loan debt than presidential student loan forgiveness. While some students seem to be holding their breath in anticipation of this, I suggest all students be proactive and avoid student loans as much as possible. If an opportunity comes to accelerate debt payoff, don't wait for the government; pay off the debt. Start living your dream life.

Student Loan Forgiveness

Another very important topic to address is the student loan forgiveness program. Students are promised repayment of their student loans if they worked in a certain field for a certain number of years and make certain qualified payments. However, many students end up thinking they're meeting the qualifications but, in the end, don't qualify for forgiveness because they did something wrong. If you're interested in a career in which your job may qualify for student loan forgiveness, it's extremely important that you work with someone who has knowledge about such things from the beginning.

You don't want to make payments on your student loans for ten years while working at a low-paying job, assuming that the rest will be forgiven, only to find out that's not the case. Additionally, many of the people in this situation are on an income-driven repayment plan. That means that while they're making very little money, they're paying very little toward the student loans. The second half of those student loans is therefore much larger than it would normally be if they had paid at a regular rate. When lawyers are on an income-driven repayment plan and find out that they don't qualify for forgiveness, they now have more than half their student loans to pay back.

It appears that the government is looking to actually make good on many who should have qualified for that repayment but failed to meet all the requirements. But, regardless of that outcome, it's best to take the initiative to work with an expert and feel secure it's being done right than to hope the government will correct any errors in your program.

Another surprise for lawyers who participate in this program is that there are tax consequences for having your loans discharged. You'll have a large tax bill that year. So, working with a financial expert who can help you plan for that can be invaluable.

If you find that you need guidance with extreme debt payoff assistance, you may want to check out Rho's podcast, Wealthyesque. Rho is a prime example of a lawyer with extensive law loans married to a doctor with extensive medical loans. After buying a home and having two children, they got serious about debt repayment and paid off their car and student loans in just over four and a half years. Almost $500,000 in under five years!!!

My husband's student loans were actually larger than our mortgage. About four and a half years ago, we added up all of our debt and we were over $670,000 in debt. I had a little over a hundred thousand. My husband had almost $350,000 and we had a mortgage that was like $200,000 and then maybe about $10,000 on a car loan. And so, all of those numbers...all add up to $670,000. So that's where we were.

Rho and her husband paid off everything except the house at a rate of approximately $100,000 a year. While they were making good money, she shares her struggles and how her husband worked "on the side" to add income and move that debt needle even faster.[15] While my goal is to help you avoid loans, if you do end up with them, learning from someone like Rho is a great way to get rid of them quickly.

CHAPTER 4: SCHOLARSHIPS

There are a few things that may have helped Rho and her husband avoid some of that debt. The magic word is scholarships. There are two main types of scholarships, those offered by the schools and what are known as third-party scholarships, and those offered by outside organizations.

One way to get a scholarship through your law school is to be an amazing applicant. If a law school really wants you to attend and someday represent their school, you may receive a scholarship. A lot of that may be based on your Law School Admissions Test (LSAT) score.

According to Sam Wolf, co-founder of Apollo Test Prep, for every point you improve upon your LSAT, there is a direct correlation with scholarships offered.[16] I will talk more about LSAT prep in a later section of this book. Just keep in mind that LSAT prep should be considered a cost-saving tool when it comes to law school and is worth investing in.

There are two reasons students spend more time on their LSAT score for scholarship purposes than third-party scholarships. First, many students don't even realize there are third-party scholarships at the law school level, and second, many students have a mistaken belief that the LSAT is really the only way to save money on law school.

While disproving the second belief is the entire purpose of The Legal Learning Center and will be addressed more fully later, with respect to third-party scholarships, they not only exist but I also highly suggest you attempt them, with a strategy. If you haven't noticed previously, everything you do when you approach law school should be strategic! It's the only way to graduate without mounds of debt.

Ashley Hill is a scholarship search strategist. She suggests you can maximize your chances of getting scholarships by focusing on local, smaller ones and by creating your own personal brand.[17] The more you know what's unique about you, the better you can convey that message and successfully obtain those scholarships!

I think for a lot of law school students, they just don't know where to start and they need the support to get started the right way. And so, if your first step is, just jump into looking, I can tell you that you're going to be frustrated because it's almost like you're looking for something, but you don't know what you're looking for. And you won't know if you found it right in the face, because you don't have a roadmap, you don't know how to get to that destination.

So, what I suggest is we have to start with you. Now I can create that profile for you, I can walk you through it on the DFY [Done For You] side, or you can do this yourself in the book [The Ultimate Guide For Finding and Winning More Money for College Now Law Edition].

I literally walk you through step-by-step... just simple things, your gender, ethnicity, what was your undergraduate college? What do your academics look like? Do you volunteer? Leadership experience? Have you written essays maybe for your, I don't know, maybe it's your college, maybe your pre-law group has a newspaper? Let's make a list of that. And then when you're ready to start searching, which will be the next step, it's only focused on things about you.

That's how you make sure that the scholarships fit you, because you're only looking with this filter of scholarships that are either - they describe you or things that you do. So that would be the first step.

And I will say too, on the other end, I get a lot of law school students that are frustrated. Maybe they started looking and kind of stopped. And then they kind of got back to it. And I can tell you that we have got to work on that too, because in-between your inconsistencies, are scholarship deadlines. And so that off week that you're not applying, somebody else is, and they're sending in their application. So, consistency is the key.

And then I'll end with this...if you started to search and maybe you're not seeing the results right now, we've got to figure out what is the hole that we have to plug. So, do you need to get more volunteer experience? Do you need to connect locally?

Considering that the cost of law school is so overwhelming, many of us freeze. We do nothing. Ashley recommends that you look at the money offered by the school and the amount left to be paid. That amount is a gap. You need to fill that gap with third-party scholarship money. This approach doesn't change the number, but it makes it feel different. It makes it feel doable.

Rather than, "I need to come up with thousands of dollars," we can say, "I need to work on that gap." In this way, if we receive a $500 scholarship, it actually makes that gap seem smaller. This is something that can be worked on while in college, in gap years, and during law school. So, get going!

I've included a sample debt reduction chart to inspire you. Can you do this without loans? If there's a large gap, how can you best fill it?

My debt free chart

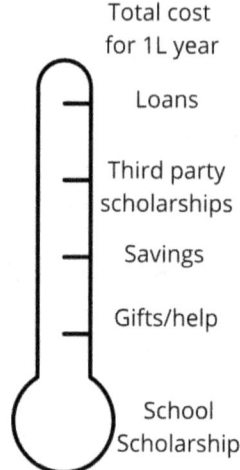

CHAPTER 5: BIG LAW MISCONCEPTION

Those who are aiming for big law may think that their student loan debt doesn't matter because they'll be making significant money. It's true that you can make significant money from day one. However, big law attorneys tend to have significant expenses as well. This inhibits their ability to accelerate debt payoff. Working 12+ hours a day leaves little time to walk the dog, clean the house, or make meals at home. And once you have children, you're going to need a more than full-time nanny. These services are not a luxury. They're a necessity so that, with the few remaining hours of the day, you can relax and have a life.

Jessica Medina is an ex-big-law attorney turned financial counselor who was stuck in that high-pay, long-hours, high-expense lifestyle. Trying to find a way out seemed impossible. It took her a while, but she figured it out and now helps other lawyers improve their finances. She knows how hard it is to take a huge pay cut, still need to pay overwhelming student loans and need to save for the future.

When you're practicing in Big Law, there's all of these different forces that you feel are out of your control, you probably don't have control of your schedule, you feel like there are all these things that you need to spend money on because, otherwise, you won't be able to live your life. You have dry cleaning, you need meal services, you need transportation, probably car service back and forth. You may need to live in a particular type of neighborhood so that you can get to work on time. I mean, there's all of these things that go along with a lifestyle of having a high-stress, high-demand job, and yes, you are well compensated for it, but if you're not watching where that compensation is going, it's very easy to just get sucked into all of that, and it's very hard to see how you could possibly survive and continue having a lifestyle that you really enjoy without that really big salary, without that comfort zone of being in an

25

industry where salaries constantly go up.[18]

I mentioned earlier that if you're going to work with a financial counselor, it's important you like their theories and style. You need to feel comfortable. Many of us already feel uncomfortable admitting how "poor" we are despite a large income. Jessica completely understands that a large income doesn't mean a large take-home check. At the end of the day, it can be just as difficult to cut expenses on that large salary as it is on a small salary. Remember, the key is seeking help so you can improve your situation.

CHAPTER 6: MONEY IS EMOTIONAL

In case you missed it from the last chapter, there is a lot of emotion surrounding finances. That's probably the main reason many of us don't want to look at our student loan figures too closely. Even if you had a decent attitude toward money before going into debt, after incurring six figures of debt, that attitude may change. It may be that different attitude that prevents you from seeking help.

Many of us feel shame or fear about our debt. Just know that the longer you wait to seek help, the longer you'll probably be in debt. Emotional spending and emotional avoidance of working on emotional spending is so prevalent that financial dignity coach Christine Luken even wrote a book on the topic.[19] If you can't even look at your loans or if you have big emotions surrounding your financial situation, that book may be an additional resource for you.

Christine completely messed up her personal finances despite being an accountant, so she knows how embarrassing it can be, as a professional, to admit that you don't know everything.

I always lead with my own story, and I am very open about the fact that I crashed and burned financially. I was actually working as an accountant for a multi-million-business, helping to prepare their budget, and yet I was bouncing my own checks at home. I had a dismal credit score. If it's possible to have a negative one, I probably did. I was in debt, I owed three different payday lenders money, and my first step in rectifying that situation was reaching out to someone and getting help and admitting, I've messed up. I need help to get out of this.

And even though I knew in my head what I was supposed to do, I didn't do it. Most of us know we shouldn't spend more than we make, we shouldn't have excessive debt, we should be saving money. Sometimes when you're in a mess, it can feel like walking into your house

27

after a tornado hits it. You walk in and everything is such a disaster, and you don't know where to start. Because it feels so overwhelming, you just don't do anything. You just slam the door and you walk away.

But if someone tells you, "Hey, look over here. You see this closet? I just want you to organize this closet today…that's all I want you to do. Don't even look at anything else. Just do this." I do the financial equivalent of that with my clients.[20]

If Christine, as an accountant, can admit to financial problems and request help, you can do it too. Don't be afraid to ask for that help! Be afraid of living in debt for years!

My goal is to help as many students as possible avoid overwhelming debt. But even if you're already in debt, I want to help you improve your financial situation. You don't have to know everything, all by yourself. And you don't have to be embarrassed or afraid to ask for help. As you can see, many professionals had to seek help before they could live the life they always dreamed of. You can do this!

<u>Part 1 Key Take Aways</u>

1. Saving money on law school is about more than just getting a good LSAT score.
2. Attorney debt-to-income ratios can make it hard to live a decent life.
3. Gap years can save you exponentially.
4. Student loan interest is 20%-80% of the amount you take out.
5. Get creative in the way you make money. Don't settle for a basic, on-campus type of job.
6. Be resourceful when you're evaluating student loans. Not all loans are created equal.
7. To win third-party scholarships, you really need to approach them strategically.
8. Don't rely upon a big law salary to get you out of debt.
9. Money is emotional.

PART 2

PART 2: SELF CARE

Between horrendous debt-to-income ratios, long hours, antagonistic opposing counsel and with everything we touch a potential opportunity for malpractice, it's no wonder attorneys have mental health problems. So, what are we going to do about it? - Jolene Blackbourn

U.S. News and World Report has repeatedly ranked the practice of law as a worse profession than nail technician, massage therapist, or pimple popper.[21] While most of us attend law school for a variety of reasons that may not be included amongst the factors in the U.S. News ranking system, the point is, we lawyers need to take care of ourselves and create a healthy balance in the profession, even if the profession refuses to do so for us.

Self-care is vital, as attorneys have some of the highest anxiety, depression, and addiction rates of any profession. To be more specific, the American Bar Association conducted a study in 2016. That study found that 28% of participants had experienced mild or higher symptoms of depression, 19% had experienced mild or higher anxiety, 21% of participants had problematic drinking habits, and 12% had suicidal thoughts.[22]

To be honest, I was given similar numbers before I ever entered law school in 1999. But I dismissed them as irrelevant to me. I had never had depression, real anxiety, nor problematic drinking. When I saw these numbers, I thought, *I'm not going to be part of those numbers because of my history. I'm going to be fine. This isn't my problem.*

Here's what I didn't know. The 2016 study only studied 13,000 attorneys, practicing attorneys. That's a very limited study in my opinion. In particular, when anxiety, depression, and addiction take over an attorney's life, they lose their license. Or they simply stop practicing and do something else. They, therefore, wouldn't be a part of this study. For this study to have accurate numbers on anxiety, depression, stress, and addiction in the field, they would need to also incorporate how many attorneys left law (voluntarily or otherwise) because of these factors. How many died because of these factors. And keep in mind that the number of attorneys who have experienced a little of these symptoms (not mild or higher as in the above-quoted numbers) is much higher.

It's no coincidence that the first three episodes of The Legal Learning Podcast consisted of people who left law fairly quickly. As you embark on your legal journey, it's important to understand why people leave law. What made them think law was the right choice and what made them think it wasn't? What was so motivating that they were willing to give up three years of their life, spend hundreds of thousands of dollars and knowingly enter such a stressful educational system? What was so wrong that they felt their only choice was to leave law? I will share the stories of Dan, Denise, Alexandria, and Megan and what you should learn from their stories in Part 5 of this book.

While many people think of self-care as diet, exercise, and so forth, it's so much more than that. It involves doing the prep work before you take on something like law school, to ensure you're on the right path. In order to avoid becoming one of the above statistics, students really need to understand what they want and how to get there. Most just seem to assume attending the highest ranked school will get them wherever they want to go. That's completely inaccurate.

The best way to ensure you avoid the pitfalls those guests faced is to interview attorneys in the area(s) of law that interest you most before you go to law school. Find out what it's really like to practice in those areas. A common mistake I see is that students don't understand what the day-to-day is really like.

Another mistake I see is not understanding what's needed to practice in that area of law. For example, in some areas of law, it doesn't really matter which school you attend. So, taking a full ride (or a lot of money) to one school may be a better decision than attending a higher ranked law school. For other areas of law, employers prefer a school that has particular electives that a higher ranked school you're considering may not have. By choosing rank over a particular program, you may be making yourself less marketable to employers in your favorite area of law.

One final mistake I'll mention is not understanding the actual income of an attorney in your chosen area of law and what your debt-to-income ratio will be. If you're interested in an area of law that starts at $60,000 and tends to peak at $140,000 but you take out the average of $150,000 in law loans, add in approximately another $75,000 in interest and whatever your undergrad debt load is, and you've got a problem. You may not be able to afford to work in your dream career and have to take a different law job. Or, like many attorneys, you may have to work a second job to make it work.

Why would you pay over $200,000 just to work any job? If your goal is to live your dream, you need to take steps to make that happen. That means conducting proper research to know what steps to take and what to avoid. Don't just assume that because you're going to law school or because you can get into a decent-ranked school, that you'll get what you want. Many students are disappointed every year. This is what I would call preventative mental health. Ensuring you live your dream.

Dr. Christian Heim is a clinical psychiatrist who focuses on lawyer preventative mental health. He has found several issues with the legal environment that leads us to having issues with anxiety, depression, and substance abuse. These issues are perfectionism and culture. The culture in the legal community is one that rewards winners, and there can only be one winner. In a lawsuit, we must win. In a case, if we're not perfect, we're subject to malpractice; our client could go to jail for life, or we could lose our client millions. And because we're perfectionists, it's hard to say, "I've had enough." It's hard to admit we have limits. It's hard to admit we need help.

Our perfectionism is really what gets us the good grades and gets us to be successful, but there's a point where it starts to harm us. Where it pushes us too far. We need to be aware of when we're crossing that line.

The stats on law students show that there's hardly any depression before law. After one year, it's like 9%; after three years, it's 40%. And there are some law schools, in fact, my son was basically told on his first day in law, 85% of you are going to suffer a major depressive episode.

So, let's talk about the profile of the person who gets into law. Your average law student has either been school captain or sports captain, was good at a musical instrument or at a sport or both, learned two or three languages, was highly competitive, was liked by all the people around them...and that all feels good.

And the nice thing is until you get to university or college, you're kind of in this safe bubble of a world where responsibility is taken by your parents, and you're allowed to be who you are. And the wonderful thing about all of that is you can be who you are, you're exploring who you are, and it feels good. And you're in this world that basically says, you know what, you've got a few gifts that other people don't have; feel good about it. You know what? You could do something like law or medicine if you want, and you go, "Oh, that would be nice." And then you start doing that. That's when things change.

And so, a few things happen when people get into law; these are people that have not failed. It's rare that they've failed the test. So, here's the first thing. First of all, you get to be a fish that gets taken into a pond with other fish like you. So, all of a sudden, you're not in the top 1% or the top 10% or whatever you happen to be in. All of a sudden, you're with a whole lot of people that were also in the top 1% or the top 10%, because all of our law students and medical students are chosen on this one, strange parameter called intelligence. It has to be that way, but it means that all of a sudden, if you're at the bottom of the class, you start to feel really bad, even though you are still in the top 5% or 10% of your peer group population for everybody in the world. But you see, you don't get to feel that anymore. You get to feel like you're at the bottom.

There are so many reasons why we, as law students and lawyers, start to lose our self-esteem, why depression and anxiety creep in before we ever face the fun of potential malpractice suits. Dr. Heim recommends we spend an hour a week just reconnecting and checking in with ourselves. This is a great habit to start before law school. Ask yourself, are you being true to you, your interests, your inner self? Think back to who you were when you were a child and make sure you're aligned with that person. This is important because if you're offered partner but aren't actually interested in that extra responsibility, you need to be aware of that and be strong in your decision. If you're not offered partner, do you even care?

Learning the practice of mindfulness can be helpful for your mental and physical health during law school (and beyond). Mindfulness means being present in the moment. It means being responsive, rather than reactive. One way to reach a mindful state is to meditate, even for a minute. Taking a few deep breaths can impact us physically and emotionally.

With all the pressures of law school and the legal profession, we need tools in our toolbox to help us survive. Metta meditation is "loving kindness." It can be done in just a minute. During this minute repeat to yourself, while taking deep breaths: "May I be safe, may I be healthy, may I be happy, may I find ease in my life."

There are classes taught in colleges and even some law schools to help students with this. If they're offered, I highly recommend you check them out. Such habits can be extremely helpful before a trial, especially if something is going wrong (like a witness doesn't show up, you forget a binder at home, your Wi-Fi isn't working).

Jeff Bunn retired from the practice of law to help law students and lawyers with cultured-centered mindfulness and meditation programs to promote well-being in the industry. The pressures of performing perfectly begin in law school with cold calls, moot court, and mock trial competitions.

What wellbeing and mindfulness and meditation do is give us strategies. The other thing is self-compassion; give yourself a break. In moot court, maybe your response isn't going to be spot on. Maybe it's not going to be quite as articulate as if we were back in our room, you know, writing the answer as opposed to giving it. As long as we credit ourselves for having done the best we can do in a difficult situation and say, "That's okay, I'm gonna give myself a little break, but I could've said this. I could have said that. I could have used this word or that word, but you know what? We did okay. We did a good job."

And if you don't give yourself a break, nobody else will, I can tell you that. So learning to give oneself a break to show oneself a little love and smile as opposed to, you know, hand ringing in the head and body and doing all the other stuff that we were inclined to do, these are all, I think, incidents of a mindfulness and meditation practice. Self-Compassion and then the ability to give oneself a break is something that is so needed.[23]

Proper exercise and nutrition are so important. They're the first things we neglect when we feel rushed and overwhelmed. Again, building habits before law school even starts can make a huge difference in how you handle law school and your legal career. Admittedly, for many of us, we lose a bit of control during our 1L year. It's hard to find time to study, attend class, exercise, and eat right. That's okay. Again, we need to give ourselves a break. But by starting healthy habits before law school starts, it's easier to pick them back up when we're ready, whether that's after one month of law school or one year.

Eating healthy and clean makes such a big difference for everything you do. So, it's not just like, "Hey, I'm training for a marathon." We've got to eat healthy, but it's pretty much like every day. And especially when you're in law school and you are just always on the go and then you're getting closer to graduation, and it doesn't end because then you're studying for the bar exam.

So, if I could go back and do it all again, I would just tell myself to relax a little bit in the beginning and find that time for myself, so that way, as second and third year come, and you're going into that bar exam, that you're prepared for that, that you've taken the time for yourself. And even when studying for the bar, I mean, those are wild times where you are just in the library, eight, ten, twelve hours a day, go into that, knowing that you need the time for yourself. So go into that already having set that schedule up for yourself over those three years so that when the bar comes, you're able to handle that stress...it doesn't get easier from there. You're at a law firm and you're traveling, you're on trial, you're taking depos. You have to find the time.[24]

Another reason to start these self care practices is to be better able to fight all the "shoulds" we're given as we enter the legal field. What are the "shoulds"?

You should go to the best law school possible (only if that will get you where you want to go)

You should be on law review (only if that's what your dream job wants from you)

You should participate in moot court (only if that aligns with your career path)

You should be happy with this opportunity (do you actually care about it?)

You should be in a study group (only if that works for you)

You should participate in on-campus interviews (only if you want one of those internships)

You should exercise, eat right, meditate, wear SPF...

Okay, the self-care stuff is great. But it's just more "shoulds." It's one more thing on the to-do list, one more failure. One more thing to feel bad about. It's hard to keep up with it all and to feel we're doing well. There are two things I recommend to counter this feeling: check in weekly with your inner self, as mentioned above, and recognize that it's a journey; it's about progress, not perfection.

I think it's especially bad or troubling in the legal industry where a lot of us are perfectionist type-A and go, go, go, hard core people and we often have a lot of trouble putting ourselves first and recognizing that taking care of ourselves isn't selfish; it's actually the best way to help us develop sustainable and successful careers and just having a life we will be happy with.

Wellness only works if it's authentic to you. What works for me is not going to be the same thing that works for you. And that's totally fine, it's more than fine; it's great.

We are different. It's important to recognize that wellness is not a one size fits all type of thing. There are many ways you can do it. If we can start to understand what wellness can look like and take that time to kinda step back and think about what our priorities are, what we want our lives to look like, what we want our careers to look like, how we can package that all together and really find some practices that help us get there. And if we can bond together as a community and say hey, we all want to be successful, we can do it together but let's make sure we sleep. It's not about working until we drop dead. These are the practices that will get us where we want to go.[25]

And speaking of sleep, consistent and adequate sleep affects our memory, our energy, long-term health and our mood. While some students enter law school with deficient sleep patterns, others develop this issue either in law school or as an attorney. Some even have insomnia.

Sleep is something that technically, comes to us naturally, but we can unlearn it. This problem isn't sustainable. Lawyers often find themselves creating forced energy in the morning (coffee), adding more forced energy later in the day (coffee, energy drinks, soda) and then needing forced calm at night (melatonin, prescription meds). Lack of sleep has been linked to depression and anxiety. Considering we're already prone to anxiety and depression, we really don't need to add to the problem.

To maximize study habits, memory and health, there are ways to relearn how to sleep. Even if you're suffering something as severe as insomnia, it can be remedied within a few months if you have proper guidance![26] The key here is to remember that law school and the practice of law can be very deteriorating to our physical and mental health. It's up to us to create and maintain healthy habits. What that looks like will vary. How well we do at it will vary!

There are more self-care tips sprinkled throughout this book. It's important, as you travel through your legal journey, that you check in with yourself regularly. How are you doing? If it's not well, why? Have you been outside lately? Have you seen friends? Have you taken a study break? Are you eating (properly)? Are you sleeping (properly)? Every day is a new day to change your lifestyle and your habits. If you need help with this, feel free to reach out.

<u>Part 2 Key Take Aways</u>

1. Law school and the legal industry can impact the mental health of all participants, not just those with preexisting conditions.
2. The perfectionism that gets us into law school can later harm us if we aren't careful.
3. It's important to be aware of our goals so we don't end up misaligned and unhappy.
4. Finding a self-care routine that works is vital - meditation, exercise, diet, sleep, etc.
5. Beware of the "shoulds" – they'll take you down paths you're not interested in and make you feel inadequate for not doing them, if you let them.

PART 3

PART 3: NONTRADITIONAL STUDENTS

First gen, gap years, learning difference, minority, female. You're not alone. - Jolene Blackbourn

The term nontraditional law student has become a bit of misnomer. The term traditional law student primarily refers to students who go to college right after high school and go to law school right after college. So "nontraditional law student" historically meant anyone who took gap years. But it also could include racial minorities and students with learning differences. At this point, taking gap years has become so much the norm, that the term nontraditional student appears to increasingly refer more to minorities and learning differences.

Although this part of the book focuses on "older" students, parents, and "differences," all types of "nontraditional" students are included in this book. You'll notice women, minorities, and first gen students throughout.

CHAPTER 1: OLDER STUDENTS

One of the most common questions I'm asked is "I'm (insert age here); am I too old to return to law school? Practically speaking, the answer is no! You're never too old. Financially speaking, the answer depends on what your financial plans are. Let's look at both factors.

As an "older" student, if you have other obligations (job, children, parents) or aren't sure you can handle the full-time program after so many years out of school, there are part-time day and evening programs. There's no need to participate in the hell that's a full-time 1L year program, unless you want to.

One of the most inspirational guests on The Legal Learning Podcast was Alex. Alex went to law school after more than 10 gap years. He wasn't sure he could handle working full time and attending law school part time. So, he tried it out before applying to law school.

So, I enrolled at… I believe it was Orange Coast Cyprus college, one of those junior colleges, and I took Introduction to Philosophy, Introduction to Logic, Introduction to Business Law, and they were at night, staggered similar to what law school would be like, and I went to work during the day, and I went to school at night; it served two purposes.

One, can I do it? The schedule.

Two, I got letters of recommendation from the professors.

So that was one thing that I did over a year period, and I said, "Okay, you know, this is something that I can handle as far as energy wise". Then I thought, okay, well, now I need to study for the LSAT. Just study.

Meanwhile, I'm saving money. I'm saving money, saving money…It took me about a year to put my package together, my applications together, write my letter of intent, my letter took me longer than anything, I was just so nervous. Am I gonna get rejected and all these kinds of things that you worry about that now you realize in hindsight, it's just all in your head.

Alex did three important things. He basically lived the life of a law student without committing to law school so he could see if he could handle it. He obtained letters of recommendation from professors. He also saved up money. While saving up money is important for everyone, as mentioned in Part 1, it's especially important if you're returning to school later in life.

Alex's advice is, even if you go and hate it, even if you drop out, you would never know if you didn't try. Don't live a life of regret. You're going to turn (insert next big age). Do you want to be that age and have a J.D.? Or do you want to be that age and still wondering if you should go to law school?

My law school class had people in their sixties. I was told there was a woman in her eighties even. Returning students even have advantages. When they enter the working world as an attorney, clients assume they have years of experience, based upon their age. The life experience of older students is invaluable as well. So don't feel disadvantaged by returning later. Remember your advantages!

CHAPTER 2: PARENTS

I'm in awe of those who go to law school after having children. After struggling through my 1L year, I have no idea how parents do it, but they do! As mentioned above, there are part-time day and evening options at some schools. The part-time day programs tend to take place while children are in school (approximately 8am-12pm). Part-time evening programs tend to take place from 6pm-10pm. These programs can help parents manage their multiple demands more reasonably.

Many parents do attend full-time, especially after a part-time 1L year. The key seems to be to know your life and understand your support system, and, of course, actually have one! What should that support system look like? It appears to be best to have at least two people you can rely on. That could be a daycare and a spouse. Or a daycare and a parent. Or a spouse and a parent. If your child is sick, daycare won't accept them, and if you have a final, you're going to need someone else to take care of them. Always have a backup to your backup!

On top of a support system, you need a system for your actual life! When will you be studying? When will you spend time with the family? Do you have time for an internship, school activities, or a club? Law school parents often do find time to engage in some activities, but, again, a lot depends on your home life and ability to get work done.

Podcast guest Lisa Lang shared her amazing legal journey as not only a mom in law school, but as someone who had her third child while in law school.[27] While the following excerpt talks about work-life balance, it's important to understand this applies during law school as well.

What I have learned is that it has nothing to do with the job that you do. It has everything

44

to do with you as a person, and you setting boundaries, because I work now for a university, and this university has students who are on campus 24 hours a day. So there are days when it feels like there is no such thing as work-life balance because... and especially with Covid, there was so much that we had to work through to figure out.

So, in some respects, I feel like I work just as hard as I did when I was in private practice. In some ways, I feel even less in control of my schedule than when I was in litigation with court orders and knowing to some degree what I had to do in order to plan for a trial, but what I would say is that experience has taught me how to create boundaries. I like to think if the supervisor is asking the question - does it have to be done now? Before, my instinct was someone says this has to get done, and then I would just put everything aside and do it, but sometimes I think it's worth asking the question - does it have to happen now, or can I take off? Because it will be there when I get back.

And the nice thing is, yes, I have job security because when that matter's taken care of, there's gonna be something right on the heels, so you have to learn to create the boundaries. Rest, relax, recharge.

The first months of law school are completely overwhelming. But eventually, you can find that balance and set those boundaries, even if those boundaries are just with yourself.

Laura started as a full-time employee, part-time law student, and, of course, a parent. She found that finding a way to disconnect between work and school was really helpful, especially on nights when she didn't have school but was trying to study. This enabled her to shift gears and really focus. For her, that "disconnect" was a nap.

Laura also had one assigned "family" day and one assigned "you don't know me" day, each week. She later switched to part-time work and full-time student. She also found time to participate in moot court. Like most students, she adjusted to the new schedule, adjusted to the new style of learning, and was eventually able to fit more into that schedule.

According to Laura, the key to success is having a support system of at least two others, understand that law school is challenging but not impossible, and be prepared to give up social media.[28] Perhaps her most important piece of advice is for the significant other of the law student.

If you're a pre-law student reading this and you have children and a significant other, let them know, just because a law student is studying doesn't mean they're OK. As students, we often forget to eat. We may be thirsty but feel too behind to get up to get water or coffee. The significant other needs to check in from time to time to see if their law student needs anything!

CHAPTER 3: DISABILITIES AND LEARNING DIFFERENCES

Students with disabilities and learning differences may face the toughest challenges when it comes to law school. Law school is very rigid and there's little flexibility for those who need accommodations. While schools technically have to provide accommodations by law, it's amazing how far they can try to push the boundaries. Depending on the school they attend, students can find themselves wasting precious time fighting their school rather than studying.

In particular, I know a student who was supposed to have a separate room for her law school finals. One hundred percent of her grade was dependent upon her finals. Just moments before one of her first law school finals was supposed to take place in the fall of her 1L year, the school advised her that they were short of staff and asked if she could "just" take the final with the rest of her one hundred classmates.

Anxiety in those moments before your first 1L finals is extremely high. Additionally, this student was supposed to have a separate room, in part, due to chronic anxiety. Yet, she found herself feeling forced to agree and disadvantage herself. This was at a school that dismisses the lower one-third of the 1L class by the end of 1L year. You don't want to find yourself in this situation. You want to attend a school that will support you.

It's important to talk to any school you're considering and find out if they're familiar with the accommodations you may require and how they handle your specific type of accommodations. Get everything in writing. Find out who would handle your needs and complaints. Talk with them before you apply and before you submit a deposit.

You'll also need to understand the school requirements. Each school is different. Some law schools have very strict attendance requirements. If you miss a few classes, you'll be kicked out. If your health demands that you rest, that you stay home sometimes, what's the school going to do about their attendance policy? How will you get the notes from that day's lecture? When will you get those notes? (You'll need them pretty much that day.)

Each professor runs their classroom differently. Some accept volunteers to answer questions, some pick on students in a particular order. If you're returning from a few days off, taking care of yourself, will the professors be aware of this and not pick on you until you've had a chance to catch up?

Are there options if you try the full-time program and find that with your needs, you would be better off in a part-time program? What's the school willing to do to ensure your success? You're paying a lot of money to attend, they need to help you have the same opportunities and experience (or as close to it as possible) as other students.

My interview with Mariette Clardy-Davis was filled with so many helpful pieces of information. I interviewed her because she withdrew from law school due to a bipolar depressive episode. She was able to later return and become an attorney. While I thought we would be focused on what her depressive episode was like and how she was able to make that decision to leave and return, we equally focused on some other learning differences she had.

In fact, Mariette is a nontraditional student in every way. She was a returning student, African American, with bipolar depression, a learning difference in speech and math, and a "different" study style.

The one thing about my 1L education is they push you further than you think that you can go. One of the things that I did realize about myself was that I knew that I needed additional support, that I would not have made it without it.

So, I did a lot of the supplemental materials, like examples and explanations. And the reason why I did those is because I was a storyteller. So, any supplementary material that could break things down like a storyteller. And I took advantage of a lot of office hours. I'm sure my professors were very tired of me, but I knew that I needed to get in front of them and ask as many questions as I could, and be honest and say, "You know what? I just don't get this," and I pushed them to make sure that I understood it. So, I really advocated for myself early. That was how I made it through. Because without that, if I would have just kind of relied on, well I'll just go home and figure it out, I would have never made it.

Despite all that she had to overcome, she was in the top of her class at the end of her 1L year! She had to work a lot harder than some others to make that happen, but she is definitely an example of what's possible.

Her bar exam study method was also unique. The typical bar exam course wasn't working for her. She realized she had to do something different. To memorize laws and legal concepts, she attached legal concepts to items around her office at work. So, her lamp may have a trigger word related to contracts. Her miniblinds may have a trigger word related to torts, and so on.

To learn how to take the multiple choice portion of the exam, she learned to answer the question before looking at the answers and then checking to see if her answer was on the exam. If not, she would eliminate the choices she knew were wrong and eliminate the answer choices in that way.

To learn application, she would read a sample essay question, read the answer and then teach the answer to an inanimate object, like a stuffed animal. This forced her brain to learn the material and how to apply it

It's so important to remember we're all unique. Law school tries to create uniformity between students. You can succeed, even if you have to fight that system and make it work for you. Don't join a study group just because everyone else is. If that doesn't work for you, don't do it! Listen to yourself, check in with yourself!

Part 3 Key Take Aways

1. Being a nontraditional student isn't so nontraditional these days.
2. Returning to school after many gaps years means being even more careful with your finances.
3. Attending a community college can help you feel more confident and get you letters of recommendation if you have been out of school for a long time.
4. Parents need a strong support system for when their children are sick and to enable them to study.
5. Students with disabilities and learning differences should thoroughly investigate their potential schools to ensure they won't be fighting their schools when they should be studying.
6. Figure out your study style before starting law school so you don't have to spend time learning it when you're in law school.
7. You're not alone.

PART 4

PART 4: PRACTICAL TIPS

Sometimes, we're so busy doing what we think we need to do, we miss the possibilities around us. Those options we ignore can make all the difference. - Jolene Blackbourn

Where would we be in a book of essentially "I wish I'd known" information if we didn't have all the practical tips that students need to know before they enter law school? There are so many different types of advisors to help you through the legal journey, but the problem is that, as students, we're so busy trying to just get through the legal journey, we often don't see opportunities and don't find the people or resources that can help us until it is too late.

CHAPTER 1: TIPS FOR PREPARING FOR LAW SCHOOL

There are sooo many ways to prepare for law school. A book full of tips just for that would be the size of a dictionary. The following tips are limited to just what the guests shared on The Legal Learning Podcast and by no means are exhaustive!

Let's start with what I consider to be a three-part problem. Part one: students don't spend enough (any) time researching their other interests, those jobs that they could pursue without spending six figures. Part two: students don't conduct, what I will call, "proper" research with respect to the area(s) of law they're interested in and how their debt will impact their ability to work in those areas of law. Part three: students don't invest in their pre-law school prep. I'll explain each of these in the following pages.

Part One - Researching Other Interests

The world is a big, scary place with way too many options. And many who are interested in law school want to make a dent in their world. They don't "just" want to be a random office worker. That's why law school sounds so appealing. As a lawyer, they can make a difference...right?

I'll get to that in a moment. But let's consider this, if you go to law school and take out all the loans, it's going to be hard to later say, "I want to be a journalist." The pay cut from attorney to journalist may be impossible to handle with your debt load. But you can certainly be a journalist and then go to law school later.

Is there an interest you have outside of law? Have you ever really thought about it? For some, this may be an easy question to answer. If you're interested in environmental law, you may simply be interested in saving the environment. If you're interested in social justice, you may simply be interested in social work.

For others, it may not be as straightforward. If you want to be a lawyer but you also like kayaking or writing, that feels a little different. But it doesn't have to be. Kayaking or writing don't have to be hobbies. They can be lucrative careers if you have guidance.

Andrea Koppell helps college students make that big, scary world a little smaller and less scary. She helps students who are stuck, anxious and over-whelmed turn their college degree into a career they'll love. In this way, students aren't left to just take the first job to cross their path. They don't feel they have to pursue higher education immediately and can instead pursue a passion or talent that they already have that doesn't cost six figures. With Andrea, they learn how to take that first step post graduation strategically.

Taking a moment to actually research other career fields or ways of approaching a career field can potentially save you hundreds of thousands of dollars! It really can change your entire life. If you find a lucrative career that makes you happy, there is simply no need to spend $150,000 or so on law school. But, of course, if you later decide you would like to go, law school will still be there. You're not giving up law school simply because you delay it. But many times, you can be giving up a simpler or entry-level career by going to law school.

The truth is, it doesn't matter where you start your career. And I truly believe now having interviewed hundreds of professionals, that your first, second, third job, they don't really matter. And you can pretty much start anywhere. And P.S. 90% of the hundreds of people I've interviewed, including me, had no idea what we were going to do with our careers. No idea. That is the norm. So, if you don't know what you want to do when you graduate, if you're kind of on the fence and you're like, well, maybe I'll just go to law school. I say, take a deep breath and do something else. And if you still, after having done one job or two jobs say, I know that the law is for me, then talk to Jolene.[29]

During my two gap years I had several different jobs. I was a front desk receptionist for a business that owned food courts. That was just to get some work experience. I then worked for a personal injury firm for three days (yes, just three days, it was that bad). I then worked for a patent and trademark law firm as a Foreign Patent Dispatch Clerk (I prepared applications to protect U.S. patents, internationally). I lasted six months there and then took a job as a receptionist for a manufacturing company for the last three months before I started law school.

That's a lot more jumping around than I had planned, but I also discovered how many horrible places there are to work in the world! I also discovered that

I suck as an administrative assistant type of worker! I honestly started to doubt my ability to handle something as complex as being a lawyer considering how many errors I made as an assistant. As it turned out, the reason I sucked was I was bored and uninterested. My experience as an attorney was completely different.

My biggest regret wasn't exploring more of my interests before going to law school. Considering I was interested in politics and nonprofits, I really should have tried to work in one of those fields. Working in a law firm that focused on an area of law I didn't care about wasn't helpful in any way.

This is the same mistake many prospective law students make. They only want to work for a law firm during any gap years. Take gap years and actually explore other interests. If the first few jobs suck, that's OK! It's to be expected while you find what works and what doesn't. Don't assume you have to spend $150,000 to have a fulfilling career. And you certainly don't have to spend $150,000 to help others.

Part 2 - Researching Areas of Law

One of the biggest problems with law school is that it's over before you know it. Most students have an internship after 1L year and 2L year and potentially one externship during the school year. It leaves so little time to explore multiple areas of law. Before law school, even if you work or intern for a law firm, they often don't expose you to what the lawyer actually does. There are a few ways you can try to beat the system on this.

Learning what lawyers do

My first recommendation is that you conduct informational interviews of attorneys in the areas of law that you're interested in. The reason it's important to do this and not rely upon Google is the same exact reason that your undergraduate professors don't let you rely upon Google for research; it's unreliable and inaccurate.

Articles about what a particular area of law is like are inaccurate because the law is different from state to state. For example, in some states, workers' compensation trials are jury trials. In other states, the trials are bench trials (decided by a judge). In some states, the death penalty still exists. In other states, there is no death penalty. These factors determine how attorneys approach trial and negotiations. You need to collect accurate information for the exact area of law and area of the country in which you want to practice.

It's also important to talk to someone on both sides of the table. If you're interested in a particular area of law, whom do the attorneys in that area of law tend to work against? Talk to a lawyer on that opposing side as well. This will give you a better understanding of what the entire area of law is like, what the differences are, and how the sides perceive each other. Sometimes, the pay difference between the two sides is vast. Sometimes, how they practice is completely different. For example, one side may be required to be in court all day, every day while the other side only goes to court on occasion. Factors like this may influence you to change sides or practice areas.

Understanding what the day-to-day job is like is so important. Many law students have no idea what a law job is like until their 1L summer internship. If a student is lucky, they intern in their favorite area of law. Even if that's the case, these students may realize it isn't what they thought and decide they don't like it. At that point, they may be $50,000 in debt and want to drop out; but how can they pay that money back if they're not an attorney? Yet, if they proceed and take out another $100,000 to complete school, they now have to find a new area of law. They may end up paying $150,000 and take any job. It's a tough choice that many face each year. An effective informational interview can help to avoid that in many cases.

Besides informational interviews, you can join LawyerUp and learn a bit about what lawyers do. LawyerUp[30] is an organization created by (at the time) a junior in college whose internship was cancelled due to Covid-19. Instead, that summer she created an amazing learning opportunity for one thousand students from around the globe. The goal of the program is to help students ensure that law is the career they want to follow by having lawyers from multiple countries speak on a wide variety of topics. These topics include interviewing skills, networking, and what it's like to practice a particular type of law. It's a wonderful program and well worth checking out before you start law school. The information you obtain in that program could save you a lot of effort within law school and possibly time and money as well.

One more program I would like to mention that can really help pre-law students connect with lawyers and get the mentorship they may be craving is Leg Up Legal. Leg Up Legal is an ecosystem of various mentorship opportunities. But most significantly perhaps, Leg Up Legal has an App that connects prospective law students with mentors who can really help students better understand what the legal industry is like.

We give you a career development plan, it has two parts, there's self-driven objectives and then mentoring objectives. The self-driven objectives help pre-law students identify what do they already know about the legal profession and what do they not know, and once you figure out what are the key pieces you're missing, then you can choose mentoring objectives that align with those to help you discover those things with your mentor.[31]

Regardless of whether or not you participate in an organized mentorship program, be sure you're always conducting informational interviews. Aside from gaining information, if you stay in touch with the people you interview, you're building your network. You don't have to do anything extraordinary. Just an occasional email; a "Happy New Year" note. An occasional hello keeps that relationship fresh. This means they may think of you when they need an intern or have a job opening. Now, rather than attending a "cold" interview where the company/firm knows nothing about you, it's a somewhat "warm" interview. You've been recommended by someone. They somewhat know you. You have a better chance of getting that job or internship. So, make sure that any informational interview you conduct, that you maintain that contact!

This was a particular specialty of one of my podcast guests who talked about some of the amazing benefits he gained through informational interviews, including several truly amazing internship and interview offers. In fact, he didn't have to participate in on-campus interviews in law school because of the internship offers he received.

I did an informational interview with somebody at Disney that was working in labor and employment, which is the field that I'm in now. I'm a huge Disney fan, always wanted to work at Disney, so it was a huge goal of mine, and I did an informational interview with several people from Disney, but one person in particular oversaw a department that I would be interested in, and I reached out to her; we did the interview.

I kept following up after. I didn't really hear anything at all, I think over the span of three years, I might have checked in six times. So maybe once every six months or so, I never heard anything back. Then all of a sudden, one day I woke up to an email from her saying, "Hey, we are hiring for a position in my department here. I was thinking about the interview that we had done a few years back. Not sure where you're at right now. I keep getting your updates… Sorry, for having not written back, but let me know if this is something that you're interested in and I can put you in touch with the right people."[32]

Definitely, take advantage of the programs that are available but conduct those informational interviews! There really is no replacement for them.

Learning what lawyers make

Aside from not understanding what their "dream" job is like, one of the biggest misunderstandings prospective law students tend to have about their future career is income (and debt-to-income ratio). They assume that the amount of loans they take out is reflective of their future income. But the reality is that many law students take out loans in great excess of what their chosen area of law can afford. This then prevents them from being able to work in their chosen area of law. It's, therefore, vital that students obtain this information in advance so that they can then only take out the amount of loans they can afford.

Students rarely make a financial plan that puts them on the path to financial success as a lawyer, if they make a plan at all. A solid financial plan should be made before choosing a law school and be confirmed after choosing one. This plan should include such factors as:

- Knowing what income they'll make in their preferred area of law (starting and later)
- Knowing how much in student loans they'll need at particular schools
- Knowing how much interest will be added on top of those loans (visit www.legallearningcenter.com/calculator to see how much you'll pay)
- Knowing how much their total debt load will be after adding in undergraduate loans and a possible bar loan
- Understanding that they may take out a bar loan and what that is
- Knowing what they will do if they don't pass the bar exam the first time
- Understanding how much debt they should incur compared to their potential income

Part 3 - Investing in Pre-law School Prep

Students convince themselves that they can self-study for the LSAT, prepare their law school applications, find ways to save money, and get good grades in law school all on their own. Or maybe with the help of their good friends on Instagram. I'll be very clear; a few people do very well with this method. But *most* of us need a little guidance in life. And that little bit of guidance can help us exponentially.

Almost every single professional who contributed to this book has worked with a coach or is working with at least one. Everyone needs a little help and support sometimes. And during this extremely difficult, transitory time of life, about 99% of students should get some help, some paid help! Those free tips on Insta are just not enough. Sure, those tips may have helped you a bit; maybe a lot, but they're not helping you reach your potential!

I know the thought of spending $1,000 on LSAT prep right before you spend $200,000 on law school may make you want to cringe. But that $1,000 will be repaid with the scholarship money you get back.

I know paying for assistance with your application seems like something you may not need, but if it helps you convey your message and present yourself in a better light, that could help you get into a school you otherwise may not have been accepted to.

I know not everyone has the money to buy all the classes offered to pre-law students. But keep these options in mind and see if there's a way you can make some of these happen for you.

There are about five different areas in which students can see huge improvements with a little investment, all before law school begins. So read through these as possible options and use what most applies to you. But remember, don't be afraid to invest in yourself.

Organizational skills

Law school is so fast paced that there's no time to "figure it out." You need to have an efficient system from day one. When and how are you going to outline? For which subjects? When and how are you going to practice self-care?

So, let's start with the basics. The skill set that helps you "get stuff done," is your executive functioning skills. Executive functioning skills are what enable you to manage daily life, and this needs to be figured out before you start law school.

Executive Functions are almost like the CEO of the brain, which is responsible for delegating tasks, planning, prioritizing, organizing, and just making sure that everything is getting done efficiently. Executive Functioning skills help you manage your daily personal, academic, and work life.[33]

If you don't have a good system at this time, it's only going to get worse during law school. My recommendation is to start finding systems that work. If you need help, figuring it all out, check out the coaches at Worldwise Tutoring. That's a major aspect of what they cover with their students. The important thing to remember is that if you don't have good life-management systems in place now, it may cause a problem in law school, and that's a problem you don't need when you're paying around $2,000 a week to attend.

LSAT

One of the first things students work on in their legal journey is the LSAT. There are a lot of ways to approach this. As you can see from this poll I took on LinkedIn, the amount of money people spend on LSAT prep varies greatly.

In particular, those who spent under $500 commented that they actually spent under $100. Many of them purchased a few thrift store books, and that was it.

How much have you spent/did you spend on your LSAT prep? Please share in the comments if you had a tutor, took a class or self studied! Tnx

You can see how people vote. **Learn more**

Under $500	39%
$500-1000	17%
$1000-$2500	33%
$2500+	10%

If you're scoring above your dream school's average, great. But most LSAT tutors agree, when they took the test, they spent way too much time trying to figure it out rather than being efficient. As Steve Schwartz from LSAT Unplugged says, "The LSAT almost ruined my life..."[34]

With focused assistance you can better understand the strategies behind the test and efficiently increase your score. Instead of studying for one year, you may be able to get an amazing score in just 3 to 6 months.

I think most of us are familiar with the standard course-style systems. Many of us took Kaplan or something similar for the SAT. For the LSAT, while that option is available, this test is much less about memorization and much more about learning what the test wants and how to apply the skills to give the test what it wants.

Sam and Daniel, co-founders of Apollo Test Prep have found one-on-one tutoring to be the most effective way to improve a score.

So, we basically created a framework where we focus on the three main skills of the test, which are finding assumptions in arguments, breaking down formal logic and doing, what's called descriptive analysis, which is basically looking at specific patterns of argumentation, looking for the general logical pattern in between. And we really believe that if you can just get really good at those three things, then you can master the entire test.[35]

Their theory is, the point of a one-on-one method is to have an assigned accountability buddy, have an expert, targeted plan based on your strengths and weaknesses and someone to explain things in a way that makes sense to you. These are all things that cannot be obtained in a course in the same way.

Sam and Daniel recommend 250 to 300 hours of study for the LSAT. They point out that each point on your LSAT could be worth tens of thousands of dollars. So don't be afraid to invest in improving your score!

If you don't want to work with a tutor, a slight variation on the one-to-one method is the course plus group mentoring method. This can provide you with more of a community while still giving you an in-depth understanding of how to approach the LSAT. I mentioned LSAT Unplugged a moment ago and this is the model they provide.

Regardless of your approach, if you aren't scoring above what your dream school would like, you should really consider getting assistance to get that score. Getting above what the school wants will get you into that school, with money.

Admissions

Your admissions packet should highlight all of your amazing qualities. It's not just about the personal statement. Many schools have personal questions as part of their application. Some require interviews or additional essays. You want to look polished, and you want to be accepted over your peers, even if you have a lower GPA and LSAT score. That's what an admissions counselor can do for you. If you have questions about the wait list and how it works, what's the best timeline for you to submit your applications and what you can expect and when, an admissions counselor will be a great asset and really relieve some of that anxiety.

I want to be clear on this. You should always use any free resources your school offers. But many times, the pre-law advisors at colleges help students navigate the logistics, such as where to find more information about the schools, when you should submit your applications and other technical information. At most schools, the pre-law advisors aren't there to perfect your application or ensure your personal statement is all it can be. They don't help you create a "personal brand." Generally, that's what private admissions counselors do.

What I try to do is kind of tour different schools to get a feel for them, get a feel for how they want to be, what kind of candidates they're looking for. And then even just the actual environment around. You're not going to be in the library the whole time. What are the job opportunities? At first people might think Brooklyn Law School, I don't know…but actually the location, the law school is in sight of three different courts - bankruptcy and federal and local and state court. So, there are all these options to intern for judges in the middle of the semester or to go and hear cases. So, I think even just that, to see how close the school is, how easy it is for you to get externships, internships, networking for jobs, all those different things that I feel like when you just are looking at the US News, you don't get that bigger picture of what the school is, what they're all about.[36]

When you're looking for a private admissions counselor, find one who matches your theories on the application process. Are they a realist? A dreamer? Will they help you present the image you want to present? Will they let you know if you're wasting your time? Or focusing on the wrong things? Can they tell you which schools will match your personality? What are their qualifications? What type of student do they best work with? These are all important questions to ask if you do hire an admissions counselor.

If you're worried you don't have the money to hire professional help, Anderson Admissions Academy was created to help low-income, first-generation, and underrepresented minority students learn how to navigate the law school admissions process and to help those students get into law school.[37] I highly recommend you consider this part of your law school budget. Save up to invest in the process and get it done right.

Saving Money

What I have noticed is that students are so busy trying to follow the narrow path that they have been told to follow, that they miss most of the money-saving opportunities available to them. Did you read the poem in the foreword? That's what I'm talking about. Even when presented with money-saving opportunities, if the strategies require students to put a toe out of line, they don't want to do it, even though it could save them tens of thousands of dollars. So please, as you approach law school, be open-minded, be creative, and remember, it's *your* path; and someone else's path (the common path) may not be right for you.

The Legal Learning Center provides tons of strategies to save money before, during, and after the application process. These strategies have been sprinkled throughout this book and are more thoroughly explained in Financially Free Aspiring Attorneys, the course that helps students save time, money, and stress on their legal journey.[38] But to give you some guidance for now, take a close look at just one aspect of the application process.

There's an almost $50,000 difference between the most expensive law school and the cheapest one. The most expensive school isn't the highest ranked and the cheapest one isn't the lowest ranked. Look at the cost of your school, the rank, and the offerings. Is there a school that costs around $20,000 a year that's somewhat similar? Could you save tens of thousands by simply looking around a little more?

Usually, our reasons for choosing a school are based upon stories we've created. We've convinced ourselves that we must go to the highest ranked school we can get into. We've convinced ourselves that we must stay in our hometown. Certainly, in some cases, the story we create is real. But most of the time, there's some wiggle room that we weren't willing to admit to. But with professional guidance, we can make a better plan or at least better see the consequences of our choices and, at least, knowingly, decide instead of deciding based upon uninformed assumptions (remember Google isn't your friend).

I can't tell you how many attorneys say, "I wish I'd known…" They say this about understanding the job, understanding their loans, and understanding their choice of school. A little advice can really go a long way.

0L Classes

There are a lot of 0L courses out there. When I went to law school, I didn't even know they existed. I still hear the same thing from current law students. A 0L course is a course you take the summer before you start your 1L year of law school. Generally, these courses will help you learn how to outline and brief a case. They'll teach you what IRAC (Issue, Rule, Analysis, Conclusion) means and how to apply it. They'll teach you what professors want on exams. They may be offered by the law school or by a private party.

I have two warnings for these courses.

First, be careful if you're comparing 0L courses. You'll be so burnt out by May of your 1L year, you don't need a course to wear you out earlier. Ask the instructor about that. Ask prior students if you can. Find out the ratio between effectiveness and energy wasting.

Second, while all students will learn some of that same information during their 1L year, I noticed my professors weren't very forthcoming. Professors would tell us what they wanted on their finals but not how to convey the information. Sure, they said to convey the information in IRAC format, but honestly, if they had shown me a paragraph from a final, that would have made a huge impact on my first semester grades. Despite their perhaps well-intentioned explanations, I still didn't understand what they wanted from me.

My grades sucked, not because I didn't know the material, but because I didn't understand how to convey it. That's actually a very common problem.

Find out if a 0L course you're considering will help you with the specifics of an exam, such as how to actually convey the material you've learned.

One last note, some schools offer small scholarships to students who attend these 0L courses offered by their school. That obviously changes the dynamic, and I highly recommend that exchange, again, if it won't wear you out for the rest of the year!

CHAPTER 2: LAW SCHOOL PROGRAMS

The traditional path has us traveling from high school, directly to college, directly to law school. Increasingly, it's common that students don't follow that path. Aside from gap years, which lengthen the educational journey, there are several ways that you can shave off a handful of years. These options sometimes come with cost savings as well.

There are about four opportunities to save anywhere from a few units to two years of college starting all the way back in high school with such options as early college high school, AP exams and so forth. Another program that's available when students apply to college or even in their first year of college, is the 3+3 program. The 3+3 program is an agreement between a particular college and law school to basically "fast track" students. It allows students to obtain their bachelor's and Juris Doctorate degrees in six years, instead of seven. It's a program in which the student spends three years in college and their senior year in the actual law school. They only obtain their bachelor's degree after their 1L year. By doing this, they save themselves one year of college.

This has the potential to save a student a year's worth of college tuition. However, it depends on the program requirements. If you're interested, you should really check the cost savings to ensure you understand it. Don't commit to something you don't understand.

There's a potential downside to this option. College is a time of exploration and fun. Committing to law school early in college limits those options and is likely to limit your willingness to explore. If you have more than one interest, you need time to try them out. If you're busy trying to cram four years of college experiences into three years, you may not get that chance. You should be open to all career paths and be sure to not limit yourself simply because a program will save you a year of schooling. If you discover a love of business or actually want to relax a little and enjoy college, do it. Law school will be there.

In the 3+3 program, you still need to take the LSAT and will actually have to do so early (before your Junior year instead of your Senior year) so that you're ready to be admitted by your senior year.

If your LSAT score is too low for the participating law school, you may not be able to continue with the program. If it's high for the participating law school, you may want to reevaluate whether you want to go to the chosen law school or examine other law schools a bit more. It's also important to research whether you would be giving up scholarship opportunities by participating in this program.

While the program will save you time and, most likely, money, it's important to remember that even if you agreed to such a program, that doesn't mean you have to complete it. It's extremely hard to walk away from something you commit to, but it's more important to do what's right for you. Priorities change and that's okay. You're not alone.[39] In fact, if you take away anything from this book, let it be, you're not alone.

Another way to shave a year off your legal education is to enroll in a two-year law school program. Again, it appears there may be a cost savings associated with this, but it's, ultimately, a bit unclear, so ask questions!

Each school that offers this program has a different approach and the opportunities offered to the two-year students are varied. In some two-year programs, students don't interact much with the three-year (traditional day program) and four-year (part-time) students. They're not always able to participate in the extracurricular activities that the other students participate in. They have less opportunity to have an internship or externship.

This type of program is certainly not for everyone. It may be harder to qualify for, as it's more rigorous. It may not provide the type of environment that you're looking for. Don't trade time for experience. Like college, law school is also a time for exploration. While there isn't as much time to explore as in college, a three-year program allows students to have two summer internships, at least one externship, and, usually, there's time to work a little. Students can study abroad and have lots of opportunities to network. Two-year programs are generally known for saving students a year but reducing or, more likely, eliminating the aforementioned opportunities.

If you're isolated in a two-year program with no time to intern, work, meet more than just the few people in your class, it will be difficult to build your network. *Networking is the most important aspect of law school.* It's how you get a job. It's how you change jobs. It's also how you vent to people who really get it. If you enter a program that's small and isolated, it's up to you to find a way to make networking happen.

As with everything related to law school, do your research! The above warnings aren't meant to imply that you should attend a traditional program. Everyone's journey is different. Priorities and needs are different. Do what's right for you. But do that research. Talk to the administration, current students, and graduates, but not the graduates the school tells you to talk to; talk to ones you find through friends or through LinkedIn. Most people are willing to spend 20 minutes with you, answering your questions about a program, even if they don't know you.

CHAPTER 3: TIPS FOR LAW SCHOOL

Building a Community

Angela Han is a life coach for lawyers and had this advice for students starting law school:

I think that the last thing that law students need is any more guilt or shame for whatever they're doing. I think that when I was in my 1L year, I just remember feeling like - How do I even read a case, or how do I even answer this question, how do I use office hours to my advantage? And I was just kind of blindly going in, not having a single idea what to do, and so I think that what I would have done in my 1L year is to hire, or at least work with or be part of a community. Somehow hold yourself accountable to the action that you want to take and get some clarity and direction on how to really maximize your mental health and your potential for your first year in law school.[40]

There are definitely ways to get that community Angela is referring to. The best way I'm aware of (and it requires little effort) is through a law fraternity (in law school, there are no sororities). I joined Phi Alpha Delta in law school, and it was the best thing I ever did. The networking is fantastic. I became friends with attorneys, students at my school, and students at other schools. I have kept in better touch with my fraternity brothers and sisters than I have with anyone else from law school. There are pre-law chapters at many undergraduate universities so you can begin your networking and involvement early if you're still in college. And by networking, I mean making friends. That's really all networking is.

New law students often feel completely in the dark, overwhelmed, and often report a huge sense of imposter syndrome. They look around and wonder if they really belong (by the way, if you got in, you TOTALLY belong, and I want you to tag @LegalLearningCenter when you get in and when you start law school with #Ibelong).

To help you feel like you belong, Angela Vorpahl hangs out with law students (virtually) starting months before law school begins extending through the end of 1L year! Angela is an ex-big-law attorney turned law school coach. While she teaches a program to help students get good grades, she also builds an online community, so students aren't alone during their 1L year.

It's important, as Angela Han says, to create community. While it's important to build one at school, building one before school starts can make the transition smoother. Having a community behind you as you start school can help you excel. So, if you're worried about feeling like you belong, worried about understanding what you're supposed to be doing, you may want to connect with Angela Vorpahl. She provides amazing content all over the internet (especially YouTube) and provides focused training for 0Ls, through their 1L year, if that's something you're interested in.

The Law School Master Plan is designed specifically for incoming 1Ls, so 0Ls as they're called. And it goes through three phases. The first phase is how to prepare for law school, all the steps you can take the summer before you start to get yourself prepared, to know what you're getting into and to know how to hit the ground running from day one.

And then phase two is the beat the curve system. So, it's all about how to use your time in law school most effectively, most efficiently, to compete for top grades, because without a doubt, as a law student, the strongest ammo that you have in your arsenal are your grades, because you don't have any substantive experience to really sell to a law firm or a legal employer. And so all legal employers will first look at your grades before they make further determinations on hiring. And so, that is the biggest piece that I want people to understand and give them the steps and strategies so that they lose no time on this incredibly big investment in time, energy and money.

And then the third phase is how to land your 1L summer job. Because there's a lot of questions around that too, in terms of like, when do I start and what are the options and what does that look like? And, I only have one semester of grades, how do I sell myself?

The idea is that it takes people all the way through the first year to know exactly what to do, and then have this process that they can then rinse and repeat to use for the second year and third year as well.

What Angela offers is a 0L course, like we discussed earlier, but with an entire year of detailed and personalized support. And she has it organized so that students don't burn out with this extra material.

I'd like to also take a moment to discuss grades. The most important grades in all of law school are your first semester grades. When you apply for internships for your 1L summer, those will be the only grades you have. Many employers judge you on those grades. Many more opportunities will be available to you if you excel in your first semester.

Additionally, some schools are ultra-competitive and have ultra-low curves. Their grading curves intentionally kick out one-third of the 1L class. If you're heading to a school like that, it's worth a little investment to ensure you're not a part of that lower one-third, regardless of your overall career ambitions, whether or not you care about those internship opportunities.

However, I also want to almost argue with myself. While the first semester grades are the most important, keep in mind the following poll that I took on LinkedIn.

Do you think your law school grades were a factor in getting your first job as an attorney?

You can see how people vote. **Learn more**

100%	40%
No ✔	38%
A little	22%

The take-away from this poll is not that grades don't matter. The point is that if you don't get the grades, it's not the end of the world. Will some doors be closed? Yes. Will it be harder to get a job? Maybe. So much depends on you, where you want to go and what else you do about it. I was able to get amazing internships/externships, regardless of my grades, which were not the best. But here's the thing, you're investing so much time, money, and effort into law school, make sure you do everything you need to in order to be successful. While you may be hesitant to spend money right before starting law school, it's probably money well spent if it results in higher grades, less stress, and a larger networking community.

1L fears

First year fears are legit. There are tons of horror stories out there. I'll share just a few with you, not to further scare you, but to show you what the reality is. Fear of the unknown is probably greater than reality. As you'll see from the following stories, you'll survive. You'll get through it.

My contracts professor yelled. All day. Every day. He never used a different voice. I only heard him yell. On the very first day of my 1L year, he yelled (of course) at the very first student he picked on. He didn't take volunteers. He chose about two students to pick on per class period and when you were done, you were done for the semester.

This first chosen student was so flustered by his screaming that she couldn't provide an answer. It was a yes or no question. He repeated his question and then began to ask if she was hard of hearing and so on. Honestly, I was just begging her to pick an answer. Who even cares which one she picks at this point? I can't recall what she picked and if she had been right. I just remembered how flustered she was. I also remember that she said her answer so quietly that he yelled at her to be louder. So, she had to repeat herself.

At that moment, I realized it was better to give a firm, wrong answer than to continue to be yelled at. So, when my turn came, this was put to the test. The night before we had read two cases that had the same facts, different outcomes. We were supposed to figure out why. I couldn't. So, I left it for class. Of course, I was picked on.

"Miss Price (my maiden name)! What's the difference between these two cases?" (always in that screaming voice)

In my mind - *Um, well, I'd hoped some other sucker would tell me.*

In reality - I'm frantically looking around for help. Everyone starts whispering to try to help but I can't hear them, since they're all whispering at the same time.

"Miss Price!"

Me - (loud and clear, remember my conviction?) "Um, nothing?"

"Oh, so you were told to figure out why these cases were decided the way they were, what the difference was, but you just threw up your hand and decided, there's no difference?"

Me - (it's kinda too late now so…), "Um, yes?" (loud and clear - plus, I was actually sitting toward the back of the room).

"Well, you're right!"

After immediately giving a retribution-filled look at all my classmates who tried to help me with wrong answers, I sat pretty tall in my seat. I learned to trust myself, my instincts and to answer loud and clear, regardless of whether

I was right or wrong.

By the end of the semester, we had all learned that this professor was actually a teddy bear. He never stopped yelling, and we didn't enjoy being yelled at, but we understood there was a good person behind that yelling.

This story is very similar to *The Paper Chase* in which a 1L spends the entire year trying to impress, really defeat his "evil" contracts professor, and, at the end, he discovers the professor wasn't out to get the student. As much as the student felt like they were personally at war, the professor didn't even know who he was.

Sometimes, we just exaggerate these "attacks" in our head. We're already nervous and make these events bigger than they really are or need to be. So, keep that in mind as you start law school. It's important to be prepared but not to let our fears run wild.

However, I want to share a more extreme example of professor behavior. I believe this professor was probably trying to weed out "weak" law students. After an event like the following, some students simply wouldn't return. For Bianca, it was fortunate that she decided to return, since she received many honors thereafter. Keep that in mind, events like these don't determine your future success.

In civil procedure, there is something called the Erie doctrine, which none of us understand, or maybe some of us, but I did not understand it. And it's one of the notoriously hard Civil Procedure cases. And this professor, basically, if you did bad on a cold call, she needed to see your notes because she needed to know what you did to prepare for her class or else. And if your notes weren't up to standard, she was going to count you absent. And at my law school, we could only have three absences per class without being deducted on our grade or failing that class. So, it was like you're going to count me absent even though I was here. So, I got called for the Erie doctrine.

And the night before I had spent five hours reading through that darn case, I did not understand a word of what it was. I still think I don't understand the concept fully, but I just did absolutely horrible in that cold call. I could not tell her what the holding was. I could not tell her anything because I genuinely did not understand the case itself. And I guess maybe that's an example of when I should have gone to office hours to be like, "Hey, I really don't understand what's going on here." But she was also a very scary law professor. She was terrifying to everyone.

So, I did really bad, and our Civil Procedure class was two hours. So, we had a 10-minute break in between. So, I did really bad; flustered on the whole cold call. And I, I guess for at least my first year, I was very scared of public speaking. And I think this is also attributed to being first gen and not really believing in your own voice. So, I was scared. I was fumbling over my words. It was just, it was the biggest train wreck that you could imagine. I want to say like Legally Blonde, whenever the professor just grilled her, it was like that.

So, during our break I was like, okay, you know what? I do not want to stay after class to show this lady my notes. Let me just get it done during my break. So, I went up to her and I was like, "Look, I read, I promise you. I read; I just don't understand any of this." I was like, "These are my notes."

"I've looked on Lexus to try and find more background info to kind of break down the holdings, things like that. Honestly, I just don't understand it that well." And then she was looking over my notes, looking through my book, seeing all the highlights and little notes that I had made. And she just turned to me with a stone-cold look and said, "Well, Miss Ybarra, if this is how your notes look, you can expect not to be here next semester," and….cue the tears. 'Cause I'm an angry crier.

So, I was like, "Oh, okay." And I got my book and I got my laptop and I put them down where I was sitting. And unfortunately, I did sit at the front of the class. So, I put it down, went to the bathroom, and cried during the remainder of the break. I think I still had five to seven minutes. So I was just absolutely a puddle of tears, I wiped my face, tried to calm down because I get very red whenever I cry. So, I had red all over my face and I just sat down with my head down for the next hour of this class.[41]

I hope you don't have to experience this! But just know that hundreds of law students go through something similar every day and we all survive. At the same time, thousands of law students don't have this problem, every day. Again, these stories have nothing to do with your success. They're a moment in time. You can do this!

<u>Important Classes</u>

Which classes are important will depend on your interests but I wanted to mention a few that have broad, practical application that you may not otherwise think about: legal technology and trial advocacy.

Legal technology

Let's start by defining terms. Legal tech can be anything, Word, Slack, you name it. This doesn't mean understanding coding, but it can. The legal industry is notorious for being behind the times when it comes to technology. Some firms still have paper files. Change is slow many times and some firms are very resistant (hence paper files).

Despite potentially entering a world of technology dinosaurs, it can be really helpful to take a class in legal technology to better understand things like privacy and privilege and security so that when you're practicing, whether you work for yourself or a firm that could use some advancements, you're working from a place of knowledge rather than ignorance.

Additionally, this can be a resume booster, even if you don't directly use it. Unlike most of your law school classes that tend to have little or no practical application to the practice of law, you can add your tech class or any skills you gained in that class, to your resume. Keep in mind that your resume audience may not be tech savvy. Colin Levy, a legal tech leader has a suggestion for this.

Instead of necessarily just listing the specific systems you've used, a list, what you have accomplished with those systems, whether it's digitizing documents, organizing contracts or just giving examples of projects that you've completed. And in the context of describing that project, mention what system you used, because I think that if you can emphasize the results and outcomes that's going make you stand out more effectively than simply just listing...so I have knowledge of X, Y, and Z.[42]

Trial advocacy

Trial advocacy is actually a required class at some schools and an elective at others. All students should take this class, regardless of their interest in becoming a trial attorney.

Not only do trial advocacy courses provide you with the communication skills that are necessary in a courtroom or in a legal forum like that, but I think that these courses also help you actually put into context some of the dark triangle lessons...with regards to evidence. And it helps with the bar exam preparation when you actually understand the rules.

One of the main skills that I think students take away from trial advocacy courses is the ability to listen, which applies in anything that we do as a lawyer. So, client intake interviews, depositions, talking to your partner, especially as a new associate, being able to hear what it is your partners want and listen to the needs of your clients. I think it's an extremely valuable tool.[43]

While some of these skills are more helpful to trial attorneys, all attorneys need to learn them, even if they never see a courtroom. For example, understanding how to examine a witness, how to frame a question so you get the answer you want, this is something all attorneys need. Whether you're using it in a deposition or to get a client to do what you want or get opposing counsel to agree with you.

Many times, a topic or issue will arise when you're talking to your client or opposing counsel and you'll need to think on your feet. How will you handle the new information you received? Practicing that type of juggling in a mock courtroom setting really develops that quick thinking muscle so you can use it later in practice.

I have certainly used the skills developed in this class a lot more than I ever thought I would, considering I wanted to be a transactional attorney. Again, it's also one of the very few classes in law school that provides students with practical skills. You really don't want that missing from your toolbox!

A further benefit of this course (and potentially the legal technology classes) is that it's often taught by adjunct professors. Adjunct professors are practicing attorneys who are teaching on the side. They're an excellent way to network! You can ask them about any bar associations they belong to or real work experiences in general. And as mentioned previously, the key is to stay in touch!

Employment

During law school, many students find time to work in their 2L and 3L years. For some, this is ongoing part-time employment with a firm. Many students manage this in addition to school and an externship (an internship for school credit). The fairly obvious benefits of part-time work include making money, gaining experience, networking, and possibly landing a job.

However, some students don't feel they can commit that much time to a job. Or they want to move around more to get a greater variety of experiences. There's another option, and this is something that's growing as our virtual world expands.

Rather than work a consistent number of hours in a physical office, students can work on virtual projects that may only last a short time. So, a student may be able to work several hours early in a semester but as the project ends and their time becomes more constricted as finals approach, they don't have to work. The next time they feel they have free time, they can work again.

By working these short-term virtual projects, students can often fit work in at night, can try multiple areas of law, and sometimes get exposure to an area of law that usually is too competitive to have a good chance of getting a regular internship, like sports law.

Attornneed calls these opportunities gigternships.[44] Several companies offer these gigternships but what's particularly special about the opportunity through Attornneed is that prelaw students have an opportunity to work with firms, which can be difficult to find. Although these jobs will be limited to a secretarial level, this could potentially create a network that the student can return to in law school.

Just remember, every time you meet someone, every time you have the smallest contact with them, intern for them, work for them; they're your new friend! They're a part of your network. What do you do with friends? You stay in touch! By staying connected, even loosely, an occasional email, a connection on LinkedIn, you're maintaining that relationship, and you never know when that may help you along your legal journey! Just because a gigternship is over, doesn't mean the relationship is.

And for recent grads who don't yet have a full-time job, this is a truly unique experience. Legal recruiters and temp agencies often want attorneys with a few years experience. Getting job placement assistance as a new graduate is hard (read: impossible)! Attornneed has opportunities for new attorneys!

Many law students never get an internship in the area of law they prefer because that area of law is so competitive. Many law students don't get a job offer before graduating and are often left to wait for their bar exam results as firms hate to hire attorneys pending bar exam results. It's a gamble at that point! But with gigternships, students may actually have a little exposure to some highly competitive fields and have a chance to work at a time when they otherwise might not!

CHAPTER 4: TIPS FOR AFTER LAW SCHOOL

We talked earlier about the importance of community. This doesn't end just because you graduate! That imposter syndrome, that feeling that you don't know what you're doing and don't know if you're messing everything up continues right on into practice. But there are resources out there, so you don't have to ask your boss every little question.

There are ways to get that support you need. Some of these options include one-on-one coaching so you can focus on exactly what you need, while others are group focused or a bit more topic focused. Just because you're a lawyer now doesn't mean you know everything! Lawyers need mentors and coaches to help them reach their potential. The following are a few really good ones!

The following are just a few of these organizations and coaches. The key is to try to recognize what you need and then don't be afraid to seek it out! Just like the recommendations for investing in yourself during your pre-law stage, it's important to invest in yourself during your career as well. The return you'll see in your career trajectory (wherever you want that to lead) will be worth that investment.

For women, Her Legal Global, run by Faye Gelb, is a podcast and blog for women lawyers and law students to learn actionable information. Faye learned, firsthand, the importance of asking yourself really specific questions about what you want to do and what you like to do to ensure you're in the right area of law. There's a long list of these types of questions you can ask yourself, starting with, "Am I a big-picture person (do I like working on bigger, involved projects) or small-picture person (smaller cases, projects that are completed and done)?" Faye also suggests asking,

How do you do your best work? Who do you like to work with? Do you like to work

alone? Do you like to work with people? How good are you at taking direction or managing people?[45]

Korey Henson is a legal recruiter and career coach. He helps lawyers find the right job through coaching and his contacts within the legal community. He works with students to figure out what they want to do so they apply for jobs that will make them happy. His view on how to figure that out comes from years of working with students.

Do you want to plan to prevent problems or fix problems because your preventers are almost always going be your transactional lawyers and your fixers are almost always going to be your litigators.[46]

He helps lawyers present their best self at interviews, which can be really hard when you're first starting out. But he also makes sure that you're happy with the interview. If you're not, even though you may really want a job, it's probably best to wait for a better fit.

As a newer attorney, it can be hard to go through the interviewing process alone; not knowing what to think about it. But with a coach who knows your values, knows what you're looking for in a career, you can stay more aligned as you go through this process.

For career confidence boosting, Emily Hirsekorn is the guru! She helps lawyers better understand how they can handle tough situations, how to better understand what to do in their jobs and what they can do to create better balance, thereby gaining confidence. Most newer attorneys wish they had someone they could ask questions of without looking stupid; without impacting their potential to get a raise. But if you ask that "dumb" question of a partner (even a not scary partner), the truth is, they may hold it against you. You never know. Is that question dumb or is it normal? Who knows? If you knew, you probably wouldn't have to ask!

Imagine having a little Jiminy Cricket in your corner. Someone you can ask your dumbest questions. Or just someone to vent to about your boss and coworkers. Sure, it's great to dump that on your family, but they don't really get it. Having been there, Emily knows what you're talking about and can help you navigate those waters to set you up for success.

If one-on-one sounds too scary, you can always join her Career Confidence Club for Entry-Level Lady Lawyers.[47]

Just keep in mind, if you feel confident, you'll look confident, and others will have confidence in you. That means, you're more likely to get the raise, the promotion, the difficult client (is that a reward?). You're more likely to be trusted. But here's the important thing. It doesn't matter if you're offered partnership faster or the big clients sooner. What matters is how you're perceived so that you have choices. The choice to move to partner. The choice to change firms. The choice to start your own firm. The choice to leave law.

Another way to gain confidence and get results is voice work. While this applies to both men and women, women are especially criticized in this arena. They're seen as being overly aggressive or meek in many cases.

Your outward presentation is one of the most important factors in your career. You can be completely competent at what you do, but if you don't exude a secure and professional demeanor, you're not as likely to get the deal, convince a judge, sway a jury, secure the client or get that raise!

Outward presentation consists of your confidence (which we already discussed), your voice, and body language (which we're about to discuss). As attorneys, we spend a lot of our time strategizing how to take a great deposition (or we should), which consists of framing our questions in a particular order and asking our questions in a particular way. We do the same for trial, from the opening statement to the closing argument. Yet, how much time do we spend working on our personal presentation?

If we come across as overbearing and offensive, with a loud voice and aggressive posture, no one wants to listen. If we come across as shy or timid, with a mousy voice and shrinking posture, no one feels they have to listen. In casual conversation, we may speak as though we're asking a question when we really mean to firmly state a fact. Doing this while negotiating or trying to convince a jury could greatly impact your case. Your entire career could accelerate if you're a better communicator. The beauty of this is that it's something you can work on before you ever step foot in law school. You can work on public speaking, before you ever become an attorney.

Rena Cook is a fabulous resource for this, as she isn't just a voice coach but one who focuses on attorneys. She has seen her client's careers take off from the work she has done with them. And in addition to actual coaching, her book, Her Voice in Law is truly a must-buy. Not only does it cover the outward presentation (voice and body) but also sales, and everything else a lawyer needs to know to be successful.

I teach a practice technique. Most attorneys, unless they bring in a focus group, don't practice out loud. They will read their notes and maybe close their eyes and look up and mumble the words to kind of get the phrase in their body. But if you do a whole practice of this speech, focusing on breathing at punctuation, that becomes the only focus of that practice and that grounds you in the breath. It teaches you where you need to breathe and you need to breathe at every punctuation. That's every comma that separates a clause, every period, question mark, colon, dash, whatever you've put in, you need to stop for breath.

Then the next run through could be for vowels. I'm just going to make more space in my mouth for my vowels in this run through. And so, I give myself a focus for each practice, which layers on my technique, so that by the time I'm ready to be in front of the judge and jury, all of that technique is supporting me.[48]

Why do some attorneys have more confidence than others? Why do some present better? While some may just have a natural talent, these skills are often taught. Some firms provide training. You may be opposing attorneys who have received this training. If you're not fortunate enough to work at a firm that provides such training and if you're not a "natural," hiring a coach for speech, for confidence, for early career skills (I'm talking your first 6 years or so), can be a career changer. When you appear confident, when your voice and demeanor support what you're saying, you'll see job offers come in, case wins, better negotiations and raises. It's fine if you don't want more trials or to make partner. The key is to have options.

Part 4 Key Take Aways

1. Law school is expensive. Spend time investigating any other careers you may be interested in that don't cost hundreds of thousands of dollars.
2. Research the areas of law you're interested in via informational interviews. Don't wait until law school to understand what it's really like.
3. Make sure you understand what an attorney in your field of interest actually makes and compare that to your potential debt load.
4. Don't be afraid to invest in you! That means possible LSAT prep, tutoring for study skills or executive functioning skills, admissions advice, 0L classes.
5. Several different programs can save you time: a 3+3 program and a 2-year law school program are the two main ones. They can also save you money.
6. In law school, building a community is important.
7. Grades are important, as they're usually the key factor to getting a 1L internship (but not the only one).
8. Law school is full of horror stories, but you'll survive!
9. Legal tech and trial advocacy are important, practical classes that will teach you skills well worth learning, regardless of your ultimate practice area.
10. If you don't want to work a regular job or need more flexibility, a gig-ternship can replace a traditional part-time job.
11. A career coach can help your confidence, interview skills, interpersonal skills, voice, and presentation skills.

PART 5

PART 5: LEAVING LAW

Just because we can, doesn't mean we should. - Jolene Blackbourn

In a book about how to best prepare for law school, it may seem a bit odd to talk about leaving law. But it's a really important topic that's not discussed enough with those just starting their legal journey. I mentioned earlier that if you have other career interests, you may want to pursue those first before you incur $300,000 in debt.

It's a lot harder to become an interior designer after you're drowning in debt than it is to leave interior design to become an attorney. And let's face it, if you're graduating from college at age 22, you have about 50 years of working life left. Can you really see yourself as an attorney for over 40 years? Doing one thing for all that time? For some, that may be great. The reality is, some of those "older" attorneys you see, became attorneys as a second career. And some of those "nonattorneys" you see in the world, used to be attorneys.

But I'm getting ahead of myself. For some, the decision to leave law starts on the very first day of law school. Only they don't actually make that decision. They stay. They suffer through. Mostly because they aren't quitters. They've never made a "wrong" decision in their life. And telling the world they're going to law school and leaving after one week seems too scary. Leaving after one year feels like even more of a failure. Now you have to quit in front of a hundred new people you met and all your old friends. And of course, if you quit after a year, you're now greatly in debt and wasted a year of your life.

There's something in the makeup of a law student that tends to say, "I don't care if I'm miserable, I can't quit." For many, there are additional pressures. They may be a first gen student, "representing" the family. They may be a minority who is determined to "pave the way" for other minorities. They may come from generations of attorneys and feel like they're letting the family down if they don't keep going.

So, the first thing I want to say, before I get any further, is that it's OK. You're not alone. And it's going to be OK. You don't have to keep going. You don't have to represent anyone. You just need to do what makes you happy. You can still help underserved communities without being an attorney. You can still make public policy changes without being an attorney. You can still learn important contract and business-related information without being an attorney. Whatever your interests, there's a way to make that happen, without being an attorney.

This topic is so important that I started my podcast, with three entire episodes of people who left law fairly quickly. Hearing these stories is so important so you can understand how and why it happens. Hopefully, you'll either avoid the same problems or, if you're debating about leaving law, you'll know you're not alone!

Meagan left law school after one year. She said that while her friends complained a lot, they agreed that she really hated law school. She was fortunate. During her gap years, she saved up and paid cash for her first year of law school. So, she walked away debt free from that adventure. I'm sure it was hard to walk away from all that money she had saved, but that's a much better alternative to walking away and having a monthly bill to remind you that you walked away.

If you kinda skimmed over the gap year advice in Part 1, Chapter 1, I highly recommend you go back and reread it. Not only can it make a difference in your future as an attorney, as Meagan discovered, it can make a difference in helping you walk away.

Meagan had some great advice for how to figure out if practicing law is right for you:

I would say, ...not only go on Google and research 'what do different types of lawyers do' or whatever, but to honestly just call up some attorneys. Most people are gonna be willing to talk to you even if it feels super intimidating, and just ask them, 'What do you do? Do you like what you do? And what's a typical day?'

Because if you're going into big law, you're going to have people that are like, 'I sleep on my couch sometimes and I'm here for three straight days', and then you can talk to somebody that is in personal injury and it's going to be way more chill. And they're all going to have their own opinions on it.

If they're doing a type of law and they've been in it for ten years, you can guess they probably like what they're doing, but it might not match up with your personality, so I would just say, talk to people. I mean, you can only Google so much, but hearing other people's real-life experience will help you get a feel for what type of law you might want to do and if you even want to be in that law field.[49]

And if you're not sure law school is right for you, her advice is:

Trust your gut, you know you better than anybody else will. Other people can only give you so much advice and so many suggestions or different ways to think about it, but I would just sit down, take a good hard look at your values in life, does law school match up with those values and what are you going to do after you match up with them? How much debt are you going to be in? Realistically, how long is it going to take you to pay that off? And is that worth it to you?

Law school is a really big investment, and is this something that you can see yourself doing for several years in the future, even though I know our generation doesn't stick with careers as long as previous generations, but in order to even just pay off loans you're probably going to be in this career for at least 10 years, so take a long, hard look at yourself and see if you're happy and if this lines up with your values is what I would say.

Meagan's right. According to another poll from LinkedIn, those who leave law, tend to do so fairly quickly. This makes avoiding extreme debt even more important.

How long did you practice law FT, if you left "early"?

You can see how people vote. **Learn more**

less than 5 years	50%
5-10 years	20%
11-15 years	25%
16+ years	5%

Alexandria Serra found herself in the same boat. She attended a year of law school but hated it. Something wasn't right. So, she left. She had completed half of law school when she left! She noted two problems with her legal journey. First, going from being a top student to being one in a classroom full of good students was hard! Second, she went from a small university in a smaller sized town in the Midwest to Washington, D.C.!

She was overwhelmed and out of her element. She had culture shock on multiple levels. She felt like she wanted to leave from day one! But she stayed for a year and a half.

Day one, one hundred percent. I felt super out of place, and I just felt like it wasn't right. And I'm the type of person that'll power through stuff. And I used to be more, I wouldn't listen to my body. I wouldn't listen to my heart. I wouldn't try to reconcile the mind-heart connection and be openly vulnerable. And so, I was just like, the only way is through; let's do it. I can do it. I'll show them. Who doubts me? So yeah, from day one. And it just was reinforced over and over and over again until I took some time off.[50]

She moved to Dallas, a city more aligned with her. After taking some time off, she decided to work full-time as a legal secretary and go back to law school part-time at night. She found that the night students weren't as intense. It's not their world. They're law students and parents or law students and workers. Or all three. The class size was smaller. Texas was also a better fit for Alexandria.

She also started in patent law and quickly discovered she was bored. So, she became a public defender, which she did for a few years before opening her own firm. Additionally, she has found that running her own side hustles keeps things interesting for her. So, keep in mind that even if you hate law school, there are more options than you would think. You can keep going. You can drop out. Or you can transfer.

This can make a huge difference. As shown in a LinkedIn post I conducted, not even a majority of law students liked their school! Considering how much money we're giving them, I have a problem with this!

Did/Do you like your law school? (Feel free to share why in comments - or not)

You can see how people vote. **Learn more**

Yes, it's great!	**44%**
No, it sucks.	**26%**
It's a school...	**30%**

If you do actually complete your degree but find yourself "stuck" as a lawyer, Annie Little helps lawyers see that the skills they have gained after law school are transferable. We don't have to stay with a job we don't like. Whether you're looking for change within the legal industry or out of it, she can show you how your negotiation skills or trial skills translate to other careers, so other employers can see and appreciate you!

She also admits that on one level, she wishes she had left law school.

My friends that left law school after a semester or the first year, I was so jealous of them. I wished I had had the courage to do that because I hated it, but I had this reason for going to law school, which wasn't great, but I needed freedom from my family. And I wanted, you know, financial independence. It was the easiest way to get there.

And I was just like, oh, good for them. You know? And then you have the whole ego thing too, like, "Oh, what's everyone going to think? I quit. Why'd she quit?" You know, that kind of thing.

But so, for anyone out there who's considering it, I'm so proud of you. Listen, you're saving yourself possibly hundreds of thousands of dollars by doing that and making that decision. And you know, I think I was also falling prey to the sunk cost fallacy as well. It's like, "Well, I'm already like thirty grand in; what's another sixty or whatever?"

It's a hard decision to make and a very personal one but don't feel you have to do it alone! I've walked through with students how to really come to a firm decision on this and how to explain it to friends and family. Because we do worry about what to say and how it all looks. The important thing is to take the time to really check in with yourself and really trust your gut.

Dan had things all worked out. As a kid, he wanted to be a baseball player or an attorney. School was pretty easy for him until he hit law school. He realized within the first month that something wasn't right. And while he knew it wasn't right, he felt stuck. Stuck by the fact that he had told everyone he was going to law school. Luckily, during law school he got an internship at a sports agency. It was the combination of the two things he wanted to do! He had found his calling.

However, he graduated in 2005 and while he got a job doing what he loved, by 2008 he was unemployed and had not taken the bar exam as sports agents don't need to do so.

A few years later, he was working as an insurance adjuster when he had the opportunity to take the bar exam and switch from the corporation's agent side to its attorney side. And while things started off great, some of the tedium of the job started to get to him. One day, he was in court, being yelled at by an opposing counsel and realized he just didn't care. So, he started to make an exit plan. He spent a total of three years as an attorney.

Dan faced what many attorneys have faced. First, he really didn't know what he was getting into with law school. Second, his understanding of practicing law was based primarily on TV, and his first internship actually showed him what he didn't want to do. Third, despite finding something he liked, he was the victim of a bad economy (the same happened to many attorneys in the late 1990s, after 9/11, in 2008, and with the pandemic - and it will happen again). Fourth, while he found a job he liked at first, the combativeness ultimately led him to leave.

Dan actually left law altogether. He is currently working as a broker and uses his legal experience to help his clients. So, his attorney experience has benefitted him, although clearly it was an expensive way to reach his destination.

He feels he was mislead by an article he read that claimed a law degree is great to get any job:

People who are not lawyers, they always say, "Oh, well, the J.D. is a great degree to have; you can do anything with it."

You hear that all the time, and that was also one thing that probably kept me going. I didn't know what that meant, but I thought, well, I might as well just have it. Because everybody says it's a great thing to have.

There are certain circumstances that I experienced where it hindered me because when the economy collapsed and I just needed a job, no one would hire me because of that, I couldn't convince these people that I didn't want to do law… I actually wanted to do something else.

I would never discourage anyone from doing it, but I also encourage, with a giant bag of salt, because you really need to know what you're getting yourself into, and if you don't know what you're getting yourself into, try to figure it out first, find that out.[51]

Remember the section about Meagan? Denise wonders if she would have become an attorney had she actually conducted informational interviews as Meagan recommended. While Denise had some general discontent in law, it wasn't until she went to an in-house firm that she saw how it could be, how some attorneys had a rhythm and flow to the practice, and while they were still working hard, they didn't appear to be constantly trying to catch their breath.

So, the in-house firm was awesome. I grew a ton, it felt like I had reached kind of a good place to grow and mature into my career, and at that point, I was like four years in when I started there, and so, it was just a great environment; I got to work with all of these amazing attorneys who've been practicing comp for years and years, like ten and fifteen and twenty years at that point.

So, I have this great experience around me, and what started happening over the years of being in this firm is I really noticed the type of attorneys who were flourishing, who had a groove and a rhythm. It was definitely a rhythm to practicing, and it highlighted that I didn't have this.

And so, I felt like I was a good attorney, I knew how to do stuff, I'm a smart person, and all of that great stuff. But for me, practicing law was very… it felt very hamster-wheelish, frankly. It took all of my energy, all of the time to be who I wanted to be for my clients and for my firm, and so… you can do that, you can push yourself, you can run, and I think any person who goes into law knows that, right, so you just do what you gotta do and you grind it out, and so that's what I was doing. But it wears you out.

And this large firm, the in-house firm, was the first time I'd really seen other attorneys who didn't have to do that to be successful. I could see the distinction of people who really have found a rhythm and a flow; it wasn't that it was easy for them by any means, but there was some flow and peace to it for them in a way I didn't have.[52]

Stories like Dan, Denise, Alexandria, and Meagan are really important so you're aware of what happens to so many students. Certainly, none of them planned to leave law so quickly when they started law school and took on those law loans. The consistent thread is that they felt a bit misled. They didn't "properly" research what it meant to be an attorney.

It's important to always check in with yourself. If it doesn't feel right, ask questions. Talk to other students, professors, lawyers, and the admins at your school. You can always take a break. You don't have to actually drop out. And keep in mind that the cultures at schools vary a lot. It's not just based on the students either. Some administrations are extremely supportive and offer weekly counseling to ensure you're succeeding. Other schools, like the one I mentioned in the disability section, actively work against students. If you're unhappy, it could be the law, it could be the law students and that environment, or it could be the actual school and the culture they have set up.

If you want more stories, Megan Smiley is the host of The Lawyer's Escape Pod. This podcast is full of stories of attorneys who have left law. Again, you may be one hundred percent confident in your choice to attend law school, but you also need to be aware of what can happen so that you can make the best plan possible. As I've said before, the best plan is to avoid debt as much as possible so you have flexibility to do what you would like in your career. If you want to change firms, fine. Work part-time, fine. Change areas of law and take a large pay cut, fine. Leave law, fine.

Megan actually comes from a family of lawyers and still fell into the same trap as Dan, Denise, Alexandria, and Meagan. Like them, she had a vague idea of what type of law she might want to do but had not done any actual research on it. She didn't really research other areas of interest either. She decided law was a nice path, and she liked school, so it seemed like a good idea. As she discovered, we can hide behind education. We can convince ourselves that our perfect job is just on the other side of another degree. Unfortunately, many of us spend way too much money on our education before realizing that we don't want to do the job that comes with that education (or not for long anyway).

So, I think when we start to ask what we want to do, a lot of us, myself included, revert to, okay, what other schooling can I get? And I would just caution people about overcommitting to degrees, because then you feel even more committed. It feels like you have made more of a commitment to something you're trying out versus just allowing yourself to say, I'm trying this out. Everyone has their path, but I would definitely caution people against solving this confusion problem with another degree.

Megan now helps lawyers leave law. But she spent time exploring before landing there. Don't be afraid to take some time, try different things out, explore!

Part 5 Key Take Aways

1. If law school doesn't feel right, don't just power through. Really evaluate what's wrong and whether you should leave.
2. Sometimes, just changing schools and programs can make the difference.
3. Lots of people drop out. And lots more want to. You're not alone!
4. If you do finish school but find yourself wanting to leave law, there are career coaches who can specifically help you describe your "lawyer" skills in terms that will be appreciated by other industries.

CONCLUSION

You may have noticed that a lot of the advice in this book is from ex-attorneys who became various types of coaches. We can all use coaches in our lives. Coaches help us reach our full potential. There really is no need to struggle alone. One of the reasons I love attorney-turned-coaches is because they really understand us. There's nothing worse than finally deciding you need help with your exercise routine and having a personal trainer not understand that you won't have access to your gym/equipment when taking a month-long trial in a small town, much less have time to use it, or seeking help on your finances and having a financial advisor ask, "Why don't you make more money?"

Ex-attorneys know the reality of what it's like to be an attorney. They're much less likely to judge us or question our "excuses." They understand the problems we face and are there to truly help us overcome them. However, a good coach is a good coach! You won't always need an ex-attorney.

Coaching aside, there are a few key points I want you to take away from what you've read here. First, lots of attorneys are miserable, but you don't have to stay that way! There are options to create the life you want. Second, one of the best ways to have the flexibility to create change, if necessary, is to avoid law loans. It's easier to take a pay cut or take time off if you aren't drowning in debt. Third, self-care is always important, so be good to yourself! Check in with yourself! Fourth, you're not alone! No matter what, it's going to be OK, and I'm here if you need help!

A list of resources mentioned in this book has been created so you can easily get any help you feel you may need at any point in your legal journey. For more information on any of the topics mentioned, check out The Legal Learning Podcast. Each guest was a wealth of information and was invited on the show to help prospective law students better understand all the ups and downs of the legal journey.

Best wishes on your legal journey!

RESOURCES

*Any items with an * means I'm an affiliate and will receive a commission for introducing you to this service, should you use them. This is at no cost to you.

**Any items with an ** means you'll get special deals if you mention that you heard about them through Legal Learning Center.

The Legal Learning Podcast
    https://legallearning.libsyn.com/
Christine Teh of Teh Financial Coaching
    https://www.tehfinancialcoaching.com/
Nick Loper of The Side Hustle Show
    https://www.sidehustlenation.com/side-hustle-show/
Sarah of Cerebellum Chef
    https://cerebellumchef.com/
Juno - Loan negotiators*
    advisor.legallearningcenter.com/juno
Rho Thomas of Wealthyesque
    https://www.rhothomas.com/podcast/
Apollo Test Prep**
    https://www.apollotestprep.com/
Ashley Hill of Scholarship Success School
    https://www.scholarshipsuccessschool.com/sss/
Jessica Medina - Financial Coach
    https://www.jessicamedinallc.com/
Christine Luken - Financial Lifeguard
    https://www.christineluken.com/
Dr. Christian Heim – Speaker
    https://www.drchristianheim.com/
Megan O'Neill – Fitness
    https://mlcfitness.com/
Hilary Samuel – Sleep
    https://www.asleepatlast.com/
Ariella Coleman – Wellness
    https://www.thewellnessesquire.com/
Andrea Koppel - Career options
    https://time4coffee.org/

LawyerUp – Internship
    https://lawyerupinternship.com/
Leg Up Legal – Mentoring
    https://www.leguplegal.com/
Student loan interest calculator
    www.legallearningcenter.com/calculator
WorldWise Tutoring
    https://www.worldwisetutoring.com/
LSAT Unplugged
    https://lsatblog.blogspot.com/p/lsat-course-packages.html
JD2Be – Admissions
    https://jd2be.com/
Anderson Admissions
    https://www.andersonadmissions.com/
Financially Free Aspiring Attorneys – Money
    www.legallearningcenter.com/financially-free
Angela Vorpahl - 0L advice
    https://www.angelavorpahl.com/
Attornneed – Gigternships
    https://attornneed.com/
Her Legal Global – Community
    https://www.herlegalglobal.com/
Korey Henson - Career support
    https://runway-strategies.com/
Emily Hirsekorn - Career support
    https://www.hirsekorncoaching.com/
Rena Cook - Vocal Authority
    https://myvocalauthority.com/about/
Alexandria Serra – Entrepreneur
    https://www.instagram.com/alexandriaserra/
Annie Little - Career support
    https://thejdnation.com

What's next?

If you're a prospective law student, be sure to become a Legal Learning Member and get notified of freebies, events, and future books!

Join our Facebook group, The Pre-Law Advisory Group.

Learn more about our courses and counseling created to help save you time, money, and stress on your legal journey.

Visit www.legallearningcenter.com for more information on all of the above.

ACKNOWLEDGMENTS

I'd like to thank my parents for helping and supporting me, my children for being the awesome beings that they are and my wonderful podcast guests and listeners, without whom, we would not be spending this moment together today.

ABOUT THE AUTHOR

Jolene Blackbourn, Esq. is a first-gen, California attorney who left her senior level position at a Fortune almost-100 company to help prospective law students save time, money, and stress on their legal journey. She also helps attorneys refine their deposition skills so they can feel confident, negotiate better settlements, and win trials. She is the mother of two humans and two dogs and loves exploring all California has to offer.

CAN YOU HELP?

Thank You For Reading My Book!

I really appreciate all of your feedback, and I love hearing what you have to say.

Please leave me an honest review on Amazon letting me know what you thought of the book.

This helps me spread the word and helps me help more prospective law students!

Thanks so much and best wishes for your legal journey!

Jolene Blackbourn, Esq.

END NOTES

[1] http://www.americanbar.org/content/dam/aba/administrative/legal_education_and_admissions_to_the_bar/statistics/ls_tuition.authcheckdam.pdf Christine

[2] https://www.census.gov/library/publications/2021/demo/p60-273.html (table D-1)

[3] https://www.nalp.org/salarydistrib

[4] https://educationdata.org/average-law-school-debt

[5] The Legal Learning Podcast - Episode 4 - When to Hire a Financial Coach

[6] https://www.cnbc.com/2021/09/01/college-graduate-starting-salaries-are-at-an-all-time-high.html

[7] https://educationdata.org/average-law-school-debt

[8] The Legal Learning Podcast - Episode 1 - Leaving the Law After 1L Year

[9] The Legal Learning Podcast - Episode 19 - Make More Money to Avoid Debt

[10] The Legal Learning Podcast - Episode 10 - How to Blog in Law School

[11] This is an affiliate link. If you decide to use Juno, I will receive a referral fee at no cost to you.

[12] https://www.pewtrusts.org/en/research-and-analysis/reports/2019/11/student-loan-system-presents-repayment-challenges

[13] https://www.investopedia.com/what-is-student-loan-deferment-4771251

[14] https://www.pewtrusts.org/en/research-and-analysis/fact-sheets/2020/04/student-loan-default-has-serious-financial-consequences

[15] The Legal Learning Podcast - Episode 37 - How to Pay Off Student Loans Quickly

[16] The Legal Learning Podcast - Episode 40 - Beat the LSAT with Apollo Test Prep

[17] The Legal Learning Podcast - Episode 36 - Scholarships for Law School

[18] The Legal Learning Podcast - Episode 12 - Financial Coaching by a Lawyer

[19] www.MoneyIsEmotional.com

[20] The Legal Learning Podcast, Episode 15, Financial Lifeguard for those Drowning in Debt

[21] https://www.lawcrossing.com/article/900049119/4-Reasons-Why-Being-a-Lawyer-is-still-a-Better-Job-than-a-Massage-Therapist/

[22] https://www.americanbar.org/groups/lawyer_assistance/research/colap_hazelden_lawyer_study/

[23]The Legal Learning Podcast - Episode 23 - Attorney Guided Mindfulness and Meditation

[24]The Legal Learning Podcast - Episode 42 - Attorney Guided Exercise and Nutrition

[25]The Legal Learning Podcast - Episode 16 - Healthy Living with The Wellness Esquire

[26]The Legal Learning Podcast - Episode 47 - Improve your Sleep, Improve your Grades

[27]The Legal Leaning Podcast - Episode 17 - The Road Less Traveled

[28]The Legal Learning Podcast - Episode 35 - Parenting as a Full-Time Law Student

[29]The Legal Learning Podcast - Episode 29 - How to Find a Fulfilling Career Path

[30]The Legal Learning Podcast - Episode 22 - Learning about Lawyering with LawyerUp

[31]The Legal Learning Podcast - Episode 13 - Mentoring and Networking Like a Pro

[32]The Legal Learning Podcast - Episode 14 - Informational Interviews for Networking and Improving Job Prospects

[33]The Legal Learning Podcast - Episode 18 - Get Organized for Law School

[34]The Legal Learning Podcast - Episode 46 - LSAT Unplugged

[35]The Legal Learning Podcast - Episode 40 - Beat the LSAT with Apollo Test Prep

[36]The Legal Learning Podcast - Episode 38 - Shoot for the Stars Admissions Advising

[37]The Legal Learning Podcast - Episode 27 - Must Know Advice from a Law School Counselor

[38]The Legal Learning Podcast - Episode 52 - How to Afford to Be a Low-Paid Attorney

[39]The Legal Learning Podcast - Episode 20 - Why I Left a 3+3 Program

[40]The Legal Learning Podcast - Episode 11 - Are You Fit to Practice - Mentally, Physically, and Professionally

[41]The Legal Learning Podcast - Episode 31 - 1L Horror Story

[42]The Legal Learning Podcast - Episode 50 - Legal Tech Doesn't Have to be Scary

[43]The Legal Learning Podcast - Episode 44 - Why Trial Advocacy is the Most Important Class in Law School

[44]The Legal Learning Podcast - Episode 49 - Gigtern to Success with Attornneed

[45]The Legal Learning Podcast - Episode 32 - Supporting Women in the Law with Her Legal Global

[46]The Legal Learning Podcast - Episode 43 - Help Your Career Take Off with Runway Strategies

[47]The Legal Learning Podcast - Episode 39 - Confidence Career Coaching for Young Lawyers

[48]The Legal Learning Podcast - Episode 45 - How Improving Your Voice Can Improve Your Career

[49]The Legal Learning Podcast - Episode 1 - Leaving the Law after 1L Year

[50]The Legal Learning Podcast - Episode 51 - Law School Dropout

[51]The Legal Learning Podcast - Episode 3 - Leaving the Law in Less Than 5 Years

[52]The Legal Learning Podcast - Episode 2 - Leaving the Law in Less Than 10 Years